Let The

BIG DAWG
EAT

★ ★ ★ ★ ★ ★ ★ ★ ★ ★ ★ ★

Let The BIG DAWG EAT

A COLLECTION OF BULLDOG TAILGATING RECIPES

Loran & Myrna Smith

LONGSTREET
Atlanta, Georgia

Published by
Longstreet Press
2974 Hardman Court
Atlanta, Georgia 30305

Printed in The United States of America
1st printing, 2003
Library of Congress Catalog Card Number: 2003100400

ISBN: 1-56352-711-1

Book and jacket design by Burtch Hunter Design LLC

To our children
Camille and Chris Martin
and
Kent and Stephanie Smith

Introduction

You may ask why I would get involved with a cookbook project? It certainly is a worthy question because there are not many dishes I know about, first hand, except for sampling them at mealtime.

Oh, I can make a mayonnaise sandwich or a ketchup sandwich, and I do a lot of that. I can even fix a tomato sandwich, and when late summer gets here, I can survive on tomato sandwiches. I even eat them for breakfast.

I can put a bowl of cereal and fruit together at breakfast, and I can grill a tenderloin. The secret with tenderloin is to cook it slowly and pour water on the meat as it is turned. Keeps the meat moist.

That's about the extent of my kitchen expertise. But the inspiration for this project came from a good friend, Joe Dabney, who years ago was a member of the sports staff at the Atlanta Constitution.

He later worked for Lockheed, wrote the history of the Lockheed C-130 Hercules, "Herc Hero of the Skies", and later came out with a delightful recipe book, "Smokehouse Ham, Spoonbread and Scuppernong Wine."

I really liked it, but what got my attention was the history of the Southern Appalachians, how they were settled and how those early pioneers could make do. They had to for survival. In conversation with one of my closest friends, Jim Minter, I asked him if something conceptually along the lines of Joe's book would have any appeal for the legions of Bulldog fans out there?

He wanted to know if a tailgate recipe book had ever been published. I checked around and found none. There have been some cookbooks by sports organizations but nobody, to our knowledge, has ever done a tailgate recipe cookbook.

There is nothing quite like the tailgate parties for college football. The fans have always gathered early before kickoff, probably dating back to the Dedicatory game in 1929—although there were not many cars in those times, very few tailgates to let down. It was a hot day and a lot of Coca Colas were sold, a record number I'm told.

You know that there had to be moonshine consumed that afternoon, too. You didn't have the smorgasbord of spirits back then in those dry county times, but there was an ample supply of moonshine.

In the late fifties I remember the tailgating scene in the old Stegeman lot, and I recall what Bill Hartman told his good friend, Louis Sohn, the year after Bill got out of coaching. After having a scotch and water with Louis at his favorite tailgate spot, Bill looked around and said, "If I had known the alumni had this much fun, I might have gotten out of coaching earlier." To which the caustic Sohn noted, "When you were coaching, we didn't have this much fun."

As time went by, I began to meet many of the alumni who gave tailgating priority, and none have underscored tailgating more than John Henry Terrell, Jr. He has made it an art.

The Kid starts planning his parties in spring, about G-Day. He goes all out and membership in his Tailgate Club is not easy to come by. Nothing means more to the Kid than to party with his Bulldog friends pre-game, then win a key victory in Sanford Stadium and return to celebrating afterwards.

There are many tailgaters with that special affection and devotion to Georgia in the Kid Terrell tradition. We thought a collection of recipes accompanied by vignettes of Bulldog football might have some appeal.

My wife, Myrna, began collecting recipes last fall and my assistant, Virna Mendoza, began organizing them and getting them ready for print. My primary job was to write the vignettes and Jim Minter provided an editing assist.

Check out the back cover for cartoonist Jack Davis' recipe. What a talent, what a Bulldog. He once did a caricature on himself, including a pot tummy. On his stomach, he wrote "Poss BBQ."

When he was living in New York, he often took Poss' barbecue and Varsity hot dogs home with him on the plane when he returned after a game.

We hope you enjoy this tailgate party book. We didn't get recipes from all the outstanding tailgaters who follow the Dogs, but I know how much Bulldog tailgaters enjoy partying. I hope the Mark Richt years will be special like so many have been in the past: good weather, great socializing and the chapel bell ringing into the night. And, if there is a recipe here that looks strikingly like one of yours, we'll take you and the plagiarizer to lunch, first come, first serve.

L.S.

Let The BIG DAWG EAT

★ ★ ★ ★ ★ ★ ★ ★ ★ ★

The Dedicatory Game, 1929

"Let the Big Dawg Eat." As this term relates to Georgia, I recall that the late Lewis Grizzard, during Herschel's time, first wrote that as another season was coming on. Then Clisby Clarke wrote a song that became a record which was popular with Georgia fans. He used that title and when you walked through the parking lots before big games, you could see the Bulldog fans imbibing and tailgating while listening to Clisby's music. Herschel made us so happy and hungry for another tailgate party.

APPETIZERS

Come partake and imbibe with us.

Jim Harrick does a pretty good job of coaching basketball for the Bulldogs, but he is a quintessential sports fan. Loves baseball and plays golf with an enthusiastic bent that is often unequaled. He likes football, too, and he keeps up with the football 'Dogs. "I like the game," he says. Harrick is one of the most knowledgeable sports fans around. And he is giving us something to enjoy in the winter.

Cheese Chile Appetizer

SALLY & JIM HARRICK

½ cup butter
10 eggs
½ cup flour
1 teaspoon baking powder
Dash salt
1 (8 oz.) can chopped green chilies
1 pint cottage cheese
1 lb. Jack cheese, shredded

Melt butter in 13" x 9" x 2" pan. Beat eggs lightly in large bowl. Add flour, baking powder and salt and blend. Add melted butter, chilies, cottage and Jack cheeses and mix until just blended. Turn batter into pan and bake at 400 degrees for 15 minutes, reduce heat to 350 degrees and bake for 35 to 40 minutes longer. Cut into squares and serve hot.

Victory Pimento Cheese Sandwiches

LYDIA & CURTIS McGILL
Curtis ('67-'69) and son, Curt ('00-'01) lettered with the 'Dogs

3 cups medium cheddar cheese
1 large jar pimentos
2 cups "Blue Plate" mayonnaise
Salt to taste
1 loaf Sunbeam white bread

Shred cheese very fine. Mash pimentos and add to shredded cheese. Add salt to taste and mix starting with one to two cups mayonnaise. Mixture should be "easy to spread". Cut sandwiches into triangles. Will make a dozen or more sandwiches.

Veggie Pizza

CATHY & CLAUDE FELTON
If there is a more capable Sports Information Director than Claude Felton out there, I'd like to meet him or her.

2 cans crescent roll dough
2 (8 oz.) packages cream cheese, softened
¼ cup mayonnaise or plain yogurt
1 package Hidden Valley Ranch dry dressing
Suggested toppings: broccoli, green onions, carrots, bell peppers (green, yellow and/or red), zucchini, mushrooms

Separate dough and place into greased 13" x 9" pan (or round pizza pan), pressing dough together to form pizza

continued

crust. Bake according to package instructions for 6 to 10 minutes or till golden brown. Cool thoroughly; combine cream cheese, mayonnaise or yogurt, Ranch dressing and spread mixture evenly over cooled crust. Top with veggies cut into appetizer-sized pieces. Complete by adding finely chopped black olives as final topping.

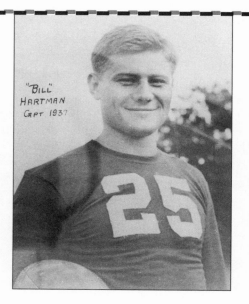

"BILL" HARTMAN CAPT 1937

William Coleman Hartman always appreciated the University of Georgia. A highly recruited high school back, he not only chose Georgia, he chose a lifestyle that would make him one of the best-known personalities in Athens. He is the most unselfish Georgia person I've ever known, when it comes to the University of Georgia. He never put his own interests before that of the school. He never feathered his nest. He never curried favor. He never sought the limelight, but he was usually in it because

of his good work and good will for the University. For years he was the unpaid Chairman of the Georgia Student Educational Fund. He was not much for beating his chest when he could have done so legitimately. He has meant a lot to the University of Georgia in so many ways. He has always meant a lot to Vince Dooley.

After returning the second half kickoff 93-yards at Grant Field in '37 for a touchdown, he lined up to kick the extra point. He was not the regular kicker and he was winded from his long run. He missed the PAT attempt and his good friend John Terrell has never let him forget it.

There have been very few things Bill Hartman has missed on in his Georgia associations.

Today, I am proud that I was in a position to be his publicity agent for many years as Georgia promoted his candidacy for induction into the College Football Hall of Fame. He made it in 1984, a well-deserved honor which means a lot to him today.

Zesty Pineapple Sandwiches
COACH BILL & MARY HARTMAN

Sunbeam Bread
Dukes mayonnaise
Can sliced pineapple
Cayenne pepper

Cut bread into circles, the size of pineapple ring, using large biscuit cutter or mug. Assemble sandwiches as usual and sprinkle Cayenne pepper to taste.

Dan Magill loves to tell the story of the days when he recruited Kim Basinger to sell Cokes at the Crackerland tennis tournament. "We sold a record number of Cokes," Dan says, "but the problem was that when someone bought a Coke, they would hang around to look at Kim and clog up the lines." The Oscar winning actress funded the erection of lights at the Henry Field Stadium and makes frequent jaunts back to Athens to see her family who lives in the Classic City.

Tuna Stuffed Eggs
KIM BASINGER

6 hard boiled eggs, halved lengthwise
1 (4 oz.) can oil-packed tuna fish, drained and finely chopped
1 tablespoon minced parsley
½ tablespoon finely chopped capers
1 tablespoon mayonnaise
1 small clove garlic, peeled and crushed
¼ teaspoon freshly ground pepper
Parsley sprigs, for garnish

Remove yolks from egg halves. Put yolks in small bowl and mash with fork. Add tuna fish, parsley, capers, mayonnaise, garlic powder and pepper; mix well.

Stuff egg whites with tuna mixture. Refrigerate until well chilled.

To serve, place eggs on serving platter; garnish with parsley.

In my book there has never been a more photogenic woman than Marianne Gordon Rogers. She grew up on Bloomfield Street, just a few first downs from the Butts-Mehre Building.

Her grandmother, Lucy Gordon, worked as a bookkeeper for the athletic association, and when Marianne came around, she lit up the athletic offices in old Stegeman Hall.

At the time the Atlanta papers published a Sunday magazine and ran a feature called "Georgia Peach." It included a bio and photo of a pretty girl. I submitted a stunning photograph of Marianne which was published a few weeks later.

A modeling agency saw the photo and got her a few assignments. She wound up as a regular on Hee Haw a few years later and when I see her today, I still consider her a Georgia Peach. She is as pretty as ever.

Quiche Lorraine
MARIANNE ROGERS

1 deep dish pie shell
1 package shredded Swiss cheese
½ lb. shaved baked deli ham
½ small onion
¼ teaspoon nutmeg
1 cup half and half
3 eggs
6 slices bacon cooked crisp
¼ teaspoon dry mustard

continued

Cook pie shell first for 8 minutes. Chop onion very fine. Heat milk and mix in mixer with eggs, nutmeg and mustard for 4 minutes.

Sprinkle pie shell with onion and bacon. Layer ham and cheese twice,. Pour egg mixture over (end with cheese on top) and allow to stand 3 minutes.

Heat 350 degrees for 45 minutes.

Easy Beef Rolls
JEANNIE & KARL HADEN

2 (3 oz.) packages cream cheese, softened
3 teaspoons onion, grated
2 teaspoons horseradish
dash Worcestershire sauce
1/4 lb. sliced beef, deli style or packaged

Combine first four ingredients. Mix well. Spread mixture on 1 slice of beef at a time. Roll beef up and refrigerate. When thoroughly chilled, the beef rolls may be cut into smaller pieces if desired. Serves 8 for cocktails.

Those who know Damon Evans agree that he is one of the sharpest young athletic administrators in the country. He is wise beyond his years and has so much going for him.

It is my belief that when Vince Dooley retires, Georgia would do well to hire one of its own who is not only capable of handling the job, but who has deep feelings and emotions for the Bulldogs. Damon played at Georgia and he has two degrees from this institution.

Who better to run the show?

Pasta Toss
DAMON & KERRI EVANS

1 (8 oz.) cooked pasta ribbons
2 tablespoons margarine
1/4 cup chicken broth
1 (8 oz.) can tomatoes, crushed
1/4 cup scallions, finely chopped
1/2 teaspoons basil, chopped
1/4 cup parmesan cheese
Salt and pepper to taste

Melt margarine in large skillet over medium heat adding chicken broth. Add tomatoes and scallions and cook until tender. Combine pasta with mixture and add basil. Salt and pepper to taste. Top with parmesan cheese.

One of the most loyal citizens in Athens is Don Perno. He and his wife, Gail, are wonderful friends. Myrna and I have the highest regard for their work ethic and generosity. Don supports everything at Clarke Central and Georgia. And the community, too.

Camille and Kent, our children, were often invited to Gail's Sunday night spaghetti suppers. They would rave about those supper outings. We all like what Don's staff prepares at Arby's.

What nice folks the Pernos are!

Olive Tapenade

GAIL & DON PERNO

2 cans pitted black olives (drained)
1 bottle roasted sweet red peppers (drained, rinsed, cleaned and patted dry)
3 large cloves fresh garlic
$\frac{1}{4}$ cup grated parmesan cheese
Salt and pepper to taste
$\frac{1}{4}$ to $\frac{1}{2}$ cup virgin olive oil

In a mini chopper or food processor chop olives and remove to a bowl. Next chop peppers and remove to bowl. Chop garlic, onion and parsley and remove to a bowl. Mix together all of above along with parmesan cheese, salt and pepper and olive oil. Add enough oil while mixing so to create a spreading consistency. Refrigerate. Serve with sliced and toasted French or Italian bread.

Brie en Croute

LAMAR & BECKY LEWIS

1 ($4\frac{1}{2}$ oz.) package Brie cheese
1 individual Pepperidge Farm patty shell

Preheat oven to 450 degrees. Thaw individual patty shell without removing "top." Roll out with rolling pin until large enough to cover cheese. Carefully pull dough over top, sides and some of the bottom. Put on a cookie sheet and bake until brown, about 15 minutes. Serve with sliced green apples that have been marinated in pineapple juice and/or bagel chips.

Creamy Tacos

TINA & TOMMY TINKER

1 lb. ground meat
2 lbs. Velveeta cheese
1 can Rotel tomatoes
1 can mushroom soup
1 can evaporated milk
1 small can of green chilies
1 can ranch style beans
1 lb. can tomatoes

Cook and season meat. In a very large pot heat all of the ingredients together. This makes a very large quantity of cheese dip. Very tasty stuff, and perfect for a large party.

Dream backfield: Sinkwich (with ball), Trippi, McPhee, Racehorse Davis. They ate up a lot of yardage.

Frank Sinkwich, Jr., is carrying on in the tradition of his father, who won the Heisman Trophy. Taking his business assets and supporting the University of Georgia and the Athens community. Frankie remembers that his late father was not only a man who believed in Athens and supported many community causes, he was an American, Red, White and Blue to the fullest.

Once when I was going to old Yugoslavia, I asked the senior Sinkwich if he knew any of his cousins who lived in Zagreb where his family hailed from? "No," he replied sharply. "Have you ever had any interest in returning to your family's homeland?" Again, a sharp, "No."

"Why not?" I asked. Frank replied, "Those people are Communist aren't they?" After agreeing with Frank that Yugoslavia had a Communist form of government, he said: "Well, I'm an American and we would have nothing in common."

Cheese Artichoke Squares
MARILYN & FRANK SINKWICH JR.

2-6 oz. cans marinated artichoke hearts
1 small onion finely chopped
4 eggs beaten
6 saltine crackers
½ lb. sharp cheddar cheese

Drain artichokes and reserve 2 tablespoons marinade. Sauté onions in marinade. Drain onion and add chopped artichoke hearts. Add eggs, crumbled saltines and shredded cheese. Mix together and bake at 350 degrees for 20-30 minutes.

Campfire Breakfast

COACH PAT DYE

½ pound bacon
2 pounds potatoes, diced
1 medium onion, diced
1½ cups (6 oz.) shredded cheddar cheese
1 tsp. salt
½ tsp. pepper
12 large eggs
Salsa or ketchup

Cook bacon in large skillet until crisp; remove bacon and drain on paper towels, reserving 2 tbsp. drippings in skillet. Crumble bacon and set aside. Sauté potato, onion, ½ tsp. salt, and ¼ tsp. pepper and pour over potato in skillet. Cook over medium heat 4 minutes or until eggs are set, stirring if necessary. Sprinkle with bacon and cheese. Serve with salsa or ketchup. Makes 6 hearty servings.

Ernie Mitchell, a native Athenian and long time real estate entrepreneur, is well known and highly regarded for his cooking ability. He designed a portable grill that not only has a grill, it has accommodations for all his utensils like pots for soups and sauces. He won't let you borrow it or rent it. If he comes and brings it, that's okay. And if he does, you are in for a wonderful feast. He doesn't have recipes. It is all in his head and when Myrna called him for a recipe, he left word on the recorder that he has no recipes.

"Just put the pig on the spit, drink for 10 to 12 hours, take it off and eat it," he said.

Football Fare

COACH PAT DYE

Spinach Cheese Squares
4 tbsp. margarine
3 eggs
1 cup flour
1 cup milk
1 10 oz. frozen spinach chopped and drained
1 tbsp. chopped onion
1 tsp. salt
1 tsp. Baking powder
1 lb. (16 oz.) grated sharp cheese (4 cups)

Melt margarine in 13" x 9" roasting pan in 350 degree oven. Beat eggs, add milk and rest of ingredients. Add cheese, onion and spinach last. Bake for 35 minutes and cool for 45 minutes. Cut and freeze or reheat at 325 degrees for 15 minutes. (these are good at room temperature and also good as an appetizer). Makes 2 to 3 dozen squares.

When I first learned about the talented Jack Davis, from his friend, Charlie McMullen, I began to discover that Jack was in constant demand as a cartoonist and living in Scarsdale, N. Y.

I got him to produce some cartoons for Georgia for brochures, billboards and football program covers. Then he contributed to a Bulldog book or two.

Jack worked hard, very hard as a matter of fact, for many years building up contacts with advertising agencies who liked his work. He has produced 36 Time magazine covers. He did the drawings, his wife Dena was the bookkeeper and they saved their money so they could some day return South. Jack is still working today, turning out cartoons and artwork from his home on St. Simons Island.

If there has ever been a more loyal and devoted fan who lived out of state than Jack Davis, I'd like to meet him or her. Jack just drools when he is around Bulldog people. He is like a kid, the eternal sophomore when it comes to Georgia.

Several years ago, I took him into the locker room at Clemson when the Bulldogs played there and he was overwhelmed. He didn't know what went on in the locker and training rooms and he was overjoyed to learn.

His cartoons are still the greatest, and I remember how interesting his work was when I first saw it. Big, long and narrow feet. The shoestrings revealed the name of his daughter, Katy, who came to Georgia and has given Jack and Dena another reason to come to Athens: grandchildren.

Grilled Devil Ham and Cheese Sandwich

JACK & DENA DAVIS

TAKE ONE SLAB OF WHITE BREAD, SPREAD MAYO UPON IT— ON TOP OF THET PUT HALF CAN DEVIL HAM SPREAD, LAY ON A SLAB OF THIN AMERICAN CHEEZE, LAY ON TOP ONE SLICE OF PINEAPPLE, PLACE ON FOIL OVER GRILL, LET CHEESE MELT, THEN EAT IT.
WASH DOWN WITH WILD TURKEY ON CRUSHED ICE.

YUM.

JACK DAVIS

Fran Tarkenton grew up in Athens, getting his athletic start, playing Little League baseball under Jim Whatley, the Georgia baseball coach. Tarkenton displayed canny leadership at a precocious age.

As time went by, he showed that he had an abundance of talent, but, perhaps, his greatest asset was that the man could lead. His teammates liked him and believed in him. It was that way at Athens High School, it was that way at Georgia and it was that way in the National Football League where he became the most prolific touchdown passer in NFL history.

Today, he lives in Atlanta, on the prestigious North side, succeeding in business which he always wanted to do. He, perhaps, has had a setback or two, but for the most part, he has enjoyed a productive and skilled career in business. All his close friends kid him about doing all those infomercials. But when ole No. 10 goes to the bank, there is no kidding.

He and his wife Linda spend vacation time in places like Hawaii and St. Bart's. They have a house at Lake Burton and Linda is the star in the kitchen big time. Fran hasn't been putting on weight, but could happen any day because he is so enthusiastic about Linda's cooking.

As often as I can get to Atlanta and find the time for lunch, I schedule a session with Foots, his high school nickname. He is pure fun to be around. He is always bubbling and kidding and cajoling his staff. He is the most positive, uplifting person I know. He is never down, he is never negative. His middle name could be "Upbeat."

What a pleasant experience to have a conversation with Francis Asbury Tarkenton, who drew up a play in the dead grass of Sanford Stadium to beat Auburn 14-13 in 1959.

Fresh Pesto Linguine
LINDA & FRAN TARKENTON

2 cups fresh basil, cut into strips
5 oz. parmesan cheese, cut into very small cubes
½ cup toasted pine nuts
6 cloves fresh garlic, crushed
2½ cups high quality virgin olive oil
1 lb. linguine or your choice of pasta
1 cup cherry or grape tomatoes, halved

Combine the basil, cheese, pine nuts and garlic in a bowl. Pour the oil over all. Season to taste with salt and pepper. Let mixture stand at room temperature for about 3 hours.

continued

Cook the linguine in boiling salted water until just tender (do not overcook, al dente). Drain and toss immediately with the sauce. Mix in the tomatoes. Place in transportable container and serve at room temperature. Makes approximately 6 servings.

Lumpia (Filipino Eggrolls)
VIRGINIA & PHIL MENDOZA
Parents of Virna Mendoza, who has rescued this author many times.

2 tablespoons vegetable oil
1 lb. lean ground pork (chicken or shrimp)
2 cloves garlic, minced
1 onion, sliced
½ lb. green beans, julienned
1 can bamboo shoots, julienned cut
2 carrots, julienned
1 tablespoon soy or fish sauce (optional)
1 cup bean sprouts (optional)
15 lumpia wrappers, square or round
Salt to taste

Heat oil in skillet and sauté garlic and onions until tender. Add pork and sauté until browned. Add vegetables and cook until tender, yet crisp, about 5 to 10 minutes. Remove from heat. Season with soy sauce. When mixture is cool, add bean sprouts. Salt and pepper to taste.

To assemble lumpia: Carefully separate wrappers. To prevent them from drying out, cover unused wrappers with moist paper towel. Lay one wrapper on clean surface. Place about 2 to 3 tablespoons of the filling near the edge closest to you. Roll edge towards the middle. Fold in both sides and continue rolling. Moisten opposite edge with water to seal. Repeat with other wrappers.

Lumpia can be frozen until ready to use.

Deep fry at 350 degrees until golden brown, about 3 to 5 minutes on each side. Drain on paper towels. Serve with sweet and sour or vinegar and garlic dipping sauce (recipes below). Makes 15 lumpia.

Vinegar Dipping Sauce
½ cup white vinegar
3 garlic cloves, crushed
Salt and cracked black pepper to taste

Mix together all ingredients. Makes ½ cup.

Sweet and Sour Sauce
¼ cup white vinegar
¼ cup soy sauce
½ cup water (or chicken stock)
2 tablespoons sugar
Salt to taste
1 tablespoon cornstarch dissolved in
   2 tablespoons water
2 teaspoons peanut butter

In a small pan combine vinegar, soy sauce, water, sugar and salt, and boil for 2 minutes. Thicken with cornstarch mixture. Makes 1¼ cup.

> *Football has always been a big man's game. That trend has intensified in recent years and sometimes I don't like it, but that is the way it is. If it was like it was a few years back, Army and Navy could still compete for the National Championship. I'd like that.*
>
> *One of my favorite little-men-in-a-big-man's-game stories has to do with the one play Billy Cloer made against North Carolina in Chapel Hill in 1965. It was a wild, high scoring game that ended with Georgia winning 47-35, getting the lead as time*

was running out. Billy Cloer (5-10, 165) gave the 'Dogs an opportunity for victory by diving into a pile-up on an on-side kick and wresting the ball away from a bigger, stronger Tar Heel to give Georgia possession at the 31-yard line. Preston Ridlehuber scored the winning points. I have always had a soft spot in my Bulldog heart for this little man who played as tall and big as any Georgia player in Chapel Hill that day.

Ham Appetillas

CAROL & BILLY CLOER

1 package supersize soft tortillas
2 (8 oz.) packages cream cheese, softened
⅓ cup mayonnaise
2 tablespoons chopped green onion
¼ cup black olives
2 (2½ oz.) package sliced, pressed, cooked ham

Remove tortillas from refrigerator. Let stand at room temperature while preparing filling.

Combine cream cheese, mayonnaise, onions and olives. Spread a thin layer of cheese mixture on each tortilla. Arrange 4 ham slices over cheese mixture.

Tightly roll up each tortilla. Wrap individual rolls in plastic wrap. Refrigerate for 3 hours or overnight. To serve, cut into ¾" diagonal slices. Makes 48 to 50 slices. Serve with salsa.

I especially like this because I can make it the night before. All I have to do on game day is dress in red and black!

Black Bean Salsa

RUNELL & MIKE CHEEK

Mike Cheek's Company, Brown-Forman makes and sells Woodford Reserve and will take his rare bourbon to the bowl game. I'll be looking him up.

2 (16 oz.) cans black beans, rinsed
2 (11 oz.) cans white shoe peg corn, drained
2 (4 oz.) cans chopped green chilies, drained
1 red bell pepper, chopped
1 small can chopped jalapeño chilies
1 small bunch cilantro, minced
⅔ cup apple cider vinegar
⅓ cup vegetable oil
Pepper to taste

Combine the beans, corn, green chilies, bell peppers, jalapeños and cilantro in a bowl and mix well. Whisk the vinegar, oil and pepper in a bowl until blended. Add to the bean mixture gradually and mix well.

Chill, covered, for 2 hours. Serve with tortilla chips.

DIPS & SAUCES

Meaty Cheese Dip
APRIL & AVERY MCLEAN

1 lb. ground beef
½ lb. hot bulk pork sausage
1 (8 oz.) jar medium salsa
1 (2 lbs.) loaf process cheese spread,
   cut into cubes

Brown ground beef and sausage in a skillet, stirring until it crumbles; drain and return to skillet. Add remaining ingredients, and cook over low heat, stirring constantly, until cheese melts. Serve warm with corn chips. Makes 4½ cups.

Tomato Salsa
GINGER HOWARD

1 fresh Jalapeno, deseeded
2 green onions
1 yellow onion, in quarters
6 cups canned chopped tomatoes, about 4-14oz. cans
1 tablespoon salt
1½ teaspoon cumin
1 tablespoon sugar
½ bunch fresh cilantro

Put Jalapeno in food processor and dice. Add green onions and yellow onions and puree. Add tomatoes, salt, cumin and sugar, and blend. Add fresh cilantro leaves and pulse a few times. Serve with tortilla chips.

Texas Chili Con Queso Dip
STEPHANIE & KENT SMITH

1 (15 oz.) jar Jalepeno Cheese Whiz
1 (15 oz.) can chili

Melt together, stir and serve hot with tortilla chips.

This recipe can be modified for those who have disdain for guilty pleasure by using reduced fat Cheese Whiz and turkey chili.

Shrimp Spread
EDWINA & DICK FERGUSON

1 carton cottage cheese
1 can shrimp
1 bunch spring onions, chopped
1 tablespoon mayonnaise
Lemon juice
Salt to taste
Paprika
Triscuits

Drain shrimp and flake with fork. Mix with cottage cheese, mayonnaise and spring onions. Add lemon juice and salt to taste. Top with paprika. Serve with crackers.

This shrimp spread is better if made on Friday before tailgate on Saturday.

Shrimp Dip

SANDRA & BEN BELUE

Sandra is the mother of Bulldog quaterback star, Buck Belue

1 large cream cheese
½ cup mayonnaise
1 cup shrimp, peeled and de-veined,
  cut into small pieces
1 small chopped onion
1 tall jar olives, chopped

Mix and chill. Delicious to serve with Fritos.

Rockin' Guacamole

CAMILLE & CHRIS MARTIN

1 1-pound eggplant
1 ripe Haas avocado (the dark, bumpy kind),
  peeled and pitted
1 red bell pepper, minced
2 mildly hot peppers (such as Italian or Anaheim),
  minced or 1 green bell pepper, chopped, and a
  pinch of cayenne
1 garlic clove, minced
½ cup minced red onion
¼ cup minced cilantro
1 tablespoon extra virgin olive oil
¼ cup lime juice (from about 2 limes)
½ teaspoon salt, or more, to taste
Fresh-ground black pepper to taste

Preheat oven to 425 degrees. Cut the eggplant in half
and lay the two halves on a baking sheet, cut side up. Bake the eggplant for 30 minutes. Remove it from the oven, and let it cool.

In a bowl, combine the avocado, red bell pepper, hot pepper, garlic, red onion, cilantro, olive oil and lime juice. Spoon the eggplant from its skin, and add it to the bowl. With a potato masher or a fork, mash the mixture coarsely. Add the salt and pepper. Chill the dip for at least 30 minutes, then serve it with tortilla or pita chips.

Makes 4 cups.

Redcoat Bacon and Spanish Onion Dip

DWIGHT SATTERWHITE

Dwight is director of the University's Redcoat Band

2 pints sour cream (low or no fat works great)
2 bottles or cans of crushed bacon bits. Or use a food
  processor to chop a pound of crisply cooked lean
  bacon very fine.
1 medium large Spanish onion (red onion)

Chop the red onion very fine and mix with bacon bits and sour cream thoroughly. Let sit refrigerated for at least one day before serving. Tastes great with any type of chip or cracker. Also tastes great on baked, or twice baked potatoes.

Pimento Cheese

JEFFREY & JENNIFER TRAPNELL

8 oz. Cracker Barrel sharp cheddar
4 heaping tablespoons real mayonnaise
Garlic salt to taste
2 oz. container diced pimentos

Grate cheese by hand (small size). Use blender or food processor to blend pimentos and mayonnaise. Add this mixture to the cheese. Add garlic salt to taste and mix.

One of the rich experiences for us each year is to spend time with Jim and Anne Minter. Jim, former editor of the Journal-Constitution, and one time sportswriter, loves the outdoors. We quail hunt every year with Don Sheppard in Sylvania, former Bulldog coach, John Donaldson, joining us. Jim has a place at the King and Prince on St. Simons and we often enjoy a cocktail hour with former Governor, Ernie Vandiver, and his wife, Betty.

Jim loves dogs, especially one on a point in a broom sage field in Sylvania. For a long time he wrote a column for his old employer for the Southside edition of the AJC. He didn't like the tension and pressure that came with it, but he wrote masterpieces like the time when he left a back door open and some goats wandered into Anne's bedroom. No columnist has ever written a funnier piece.

Jim and Anne are avid Bulldog fans, holding season tickets and trekking to most out of town games.

But Jim thinks college football is killing the golden goose. He didn't go to the Florida game in Jacksonville this year.

"Playing that game at night is disgusting," he says. "Greed got Enron, WorldCom, Arthur Anderson and Imclone. Can college athletics be far behind?"

Unfortunately, a lot of folks agree with Jim. Let's not ruin a wonderful game over money.

Pimento Cheese Spread

ANNE & JIM MINTER

16 oz. sharp cheddar cheese, finely grated
1 8oz. package cream cheese, softened
    to room temperature
1 ½ cup Hellman's mayonnaise
½ cup sour cream
1 4oz. jar chopped pimentos, undrained

In a medium bowl, mix cheeses with mayonnaise, sour cream, and pimentos, stirring until combined. Store in refrigerator. It will keep several weeks. For variety add chopped jalapeno peppers or olives.

Pimento Cheese Spread or Dip
GAIL ROBERTSON

2 cups grated cheese, whatever kind you like, I use ½
　　sharp and ½ medium cheddar
Large jar drained pimentos
Salt and pepper to taste
2 tablespoons sour cream
3 tablespoons mayonnaise

Mexican Dip
DEBBIE & CHARLEY WHITTEMORE
Charley lettered with the Bulldogs 1968-70
and is one of the hardest workers on the Bulldog athletic staff today

2 cans bean dip
1 (8 oz.) sour cream
1 package taco mix
½ cup mayonnaise
Chopped green onions
Chopped tomatoes
Chopped (or sliced) black olives
Grated cheese

In a shallow pie plate or baking dish, spread the two cans of bean dip. Mix together sour cream, taco mix and mayonnaise. Spread the mixture on top of the bean dip.

Layer each of the following four ingredients in order. Refrigerate for several hours before serving. Serve with tortilla chips.

Black Olive Dip
STUART & JAN SATTERFIELD

1 large can pitted black olives
2 large tomatoes, chopped
3 to 4 green onions, chopped
3 to 4 jalapeño peppers, seeded and chopped
3 tablespoons vinegar
1 clove garlic or 1 tsp. garlic salt or powder
Salt and pepper to taste

Chop the green onions and tomato by hand. Chop the olive, jalapeño and garlic in food processor. Let stand 3 to 4 hours before serving. Drain the juice and serve with tostado chips.

Mexican Dip
BARBARA & DON HEMRICK

1 can black beans
1 small can white shoe peg corn
1 large jar Pace medium hot salsa
½ package (or to suit) Mexican 3 cheese
Fresh cilantro, if desired

Rinse black beans and drain. Drain corn. Mix all ingredients together and serve with Tostidos.

Hot Artichoke Dip
JEFFREY & JENNIFER TRAPNELL

1 (8 oz.) can artichoke hearts
1 (6 oz.) jar of marinated artichoke hearts
6 tablespoons real mayonnaise
1 (4 oz.) can diced green chilies
Salt and pepper
2 cups shredded cheddar cheese

Drain marinated artichoke hearts and reserve 3 tablespoons of the marinade. Using a blender or food processor, blend artichoke hearts and green chilies. Add in mayo, salt and pepper (to taste). Pour into greased 9-inch pie plate. Top with cheddar cheese. Bake at 350 degrees for 20-30 minutes. Serve with tortilla chips.

Crawfish, Shrimp or Crab Dip
NANCY & GARY COUVILLON

1 stick butter
1 chopped onion
1 chopped bell pepper
1 tbs. chopped garlic
1 lb. Seafood of choice
1 can cream of mushroom soup
Tony Cachere's seasoning to taste.
Worcestershire sauce to taste
Tabasco sauce to taste

Cook onion, bell pepper and garlic in butter. Add seafood and cook for 20 minutes. Remove from burner. Add soup. Add seasonings and mix well. Make one day ahead. Serve with melba rounds or crackers.

BLT Dip
SHANNON & ED FERGUSON

1 cup mayonnaise
1 cup sour cream
10 pieces bacon crumbled
1 tomato chopped

Mix sour cream, mayonnaise and bacon and top with chopped tomato. Serve on a bed of green leaf lettuce with Ritz crackers.

Apple Dip
BILL & NAN O'LEARY

6 apples
8 oz. softened cream cheese
1 cup confectioners sugar

Mix and spread in bottom of quiche pan. Top with Marzetti's caramel apple dip. Use Sprite to retain color on apples. Pour Sprite in bowl. Place apple slices in Sprite 1 to 2 minutes. Then place apple slices on paper towel and pat dry. Arrange apples on platter and for holidays, use red and green apples.

Mexican Dip
COACH JOHNNY GRIFFITH

1 can Frito Lay bean dip
1 tub guacamole dip
1 can Frito Lay onion dip
1 small jar salsa
1 can sliced black olives
1 cup fresh diced tomatoes
6 to 8 oz. grated Colby cheese
6 to 8 oz. grated Monterey Jack cheese
1 bunch sliced spring onion (optional)
1 can green chili pepper (optional)

Layer ingredients and refrigerate for several hours. May add dollops of sour cream, if desired. Serve with "Scoop" Frito Lay chips.

Artichoke Spinach Dip
ANDREA & JOHN WITHERS

1 can artichoke hearts, drained and cut up
1 can Rotel tomatoes and green chilies, drained
1 cup parmesan cheese
1 package frozen spinach, thawed and drained but
    not cooked
½ cup light mayonnaise
½ cup light or nonfat sour cream

Mix all together and put in quiche pan. Bake at 350 degrees for about 25 to 30 minutes. Serve with Tostidos.

Artichoke Dip
SUE & JACK BUSH
Jack Bush was starting tackle on the undefeated Bulldogs of 1946

1 large can hearts of artichoke or 2 small jars
1 small onion chopped fine
¾ cup mayonnaise
Dash of Worcestershire sauce
Parmesan cheese to garnish

Drain artichokes and mash. Mix next 3 ingredients, bake at 350 degrees until cheese is brown on top, approximately 20 to 30 minutes.
    This is better served warm but may also be served cold.

Marinade for Grilled Salmon
KAREN & JIM HOLBROOK
Karen is now the President of Ohio State University. She was provost at UGA.

¼ cup butter, melted but not hot
1 clove garlic, minced (or garlic salt to taste)
¼ cup ketchup
¼ cup soy sauce
2 tablespoons mustard
Dash Worcestershire sauce
Dash pepper
1 tablespoon lemon juice (optional)

Combine all ingredients and heat, but do not boil. Ask the fish store to filet a whole salmon, and spread the sauce on non-skin side of salmon just before grilling. I often marinate salmon in the sauce in the refrigerator a few hours before grilling.

E. H. Culpepper not only loves the Dogs, he loves the University, Athens and the state of Georgia. And he is always trying to promote goodwill for his favorite institutions.

E.H. has midwifed countless ideas for our community. He is a dreamer and he is the most enthusiastic unpaid ambassador Athens and Clarke County has ever had.

He spends every waking hour trying to do good for something or somebody. He's the unofficial mayor of the Civic Center and when somebody needs anything, he is the man on call. He can answer your question, he will host a tour and he'll do whatever is necessary to accommodate any visitor or guest. He can show off Athens better than a grandmother can show off her first-born grandchild.

And he cooks the best ribs.

Cool's Barbeque Sauce

E.H. & KITTY CULPEPPER

3 cups vinegar
1½ cups ketchup
2 tablespoons sugar
2 tablespoons Heinz 57
2 tablespoons Worcestershire sauce
½ lemon
1 stick of butter
1 teaspoon pepper, 1 teaspoon salt
½ cup beer or Coke

Begin with top 5 ingredients and then add balance of ingredients. Simmer for 30 minutes. Do not let it come to a boil.

I love Dan Magill. He was my mentor when I came to the campus. He has been my best friend, he has been my promoter and my confidante. There is nobody I admire or respect more. He has demonstrated forever that he truly loves the University. An Athens boy, he has done and is doing exactly what he always wanted to do. He never made a lot of money, he never accumulated wealth and assets. "But," he says, "I have had a wonderful life living in Athens and having an association with the University."

His life was a six and a half day week. He left the office at noon on Sunday to head home to do yard work or to the tennis courts. When he turned 80, he still worked in his yard and still played tennis. He is my hero, my inspiration and still, fortunately, my beer drinking buddy. When I am in town, we, at least twice a week, head up to Hugh Acheson's delightful place, "The Five and Ten," for a few beers.

It is a session of humor, nonsensical chatter, blue jokes, bawdy limericks, reminiscences, cynical viewpoints, hilarity. We talk about Georgia athletic history, the Braves to which we are devoted fans, we share our thoughts on World War II and we gripe about the lack of respect that seems to permeate our world. People don't seem to honor flag and country like in the past. But sadly, we agree, that 9-11 brought about a renewal of patriotism.

None of our sessions are without some antipathy expressed for Georgia Tech. Dan, who suffered through an eight-year drought with the Jackets, relishes any success against the archenemy. In 1959 when Georgia came back in the closing seconds to *edge Auburn, 14-13 to win the SEC championship, there was plenty of cheering in the Sanford Stadium press box. Tech was playing in Tuscaloosa that afternoon and the Western Union ticker brought the news that Alabama had upset the Jackets. Dan jumped up on a bench in the old press box and screamed, "Doubleheader."*

Old McWhorter Barbeque Sauce
ROSEMARY & DAN MAGILL

½ pound butter (2 sticks)
11 cup vinegar
1 tsp. each:
Black pepper
Red pepper
Salt
Dry mustard
4 tbs. tomato catsup
Dash of Worchestshire

Simmer until mixed. Pour over chicken breasts or whatever you're cooking. Cook in 325 oven until done (30 minutes or more). This sauce can be refrigerated and heated later.

For years Judd and Betty Farr of Greenville drove a converted bus, which they painted red and black and turned into a kitchen on wheels. Each week they barbecued 250 pieces of chicken for Bulldog

games. They had to start cooking Friday morning.

Every Saturday the bus was parked across from the Stegeman lot and, in addition to their friends and guests, the cheerleaders came by – even opposing cheerleaders. No wonder, the eatin' was as good as you could imagine (their daughters, Gena and Amy, were members of the Bulldog cheering squad).

Their tailgate parties (even on the road where there was, understandably less hospitality than in Athens) were an example of what college football is, or should be. Fight it out on the field but tailgate before and after the game without fuss, rancor or ill will. The Farrs did it the way it should be done.

Judd is a Georgia graduate, class of '49. He lettered in basketball and track, setting the high jump record in '48 that stood for 10 years. He has retired the big red and black party wagon, but he and Betty are still on hand when the 'Dogs take the field.

Judd's Famous Chicken Sauce
JUDD & BETTY FARR

3 qts. White House apple vinegar
1½ cups salt
¼ cup black pepper
¼ cup paprika
½ cup crushed red pepper
2 cups Wesson oil
1 cup Worcestershire sauce

Shake well before each use. Dash on chicken repeatedly while cooking.

SOUPS & CHILIS

QB Kirby Moore passes...

...to TE Pat Hodgson...

...who pitches back...

...to Bob Taylor...

...who scores on 73-yd TD.

Moore to Hodgson to Taylor ... to glory.
—Dan Magill, 8:15 A.M., September 19, 1965

Wild Duck Creole

BOB TAYLOR

Letterman 1963-65, Bob scored on the flea flicker to upset Alabama in 1965

1 medium duck
1 medium onion, chopped
2 stalks celery, chopped
1 bud garlic
Salt and pepper
Soy sauce
3 tablespoons bacon fat
1 cup water
1 chicken bouillon cube
1 small can tomato sauce

Clean duck, wipe almost dry. Rub inside and out with salt and pepper. Rub outside with soy sauce and bacon fat. Brown duck on all sides in Dutch oven. Remove duck from pan; add onion, celery and garlic; cook until wilted and tender. Return duck, liver and gizzard to pan. Add water, bouillon cube and tomato sauce. Cover and cook three hours in a 325 to 350 degree oven. Add chopped giblets to gravy. Will serve 3 to 4 people.

Gator Stew

MICHELE CLOVIS

Gator tail meat, stewed veges (carrots, corn kernel, potato, shallots, onions)

Steam gator to tenderize, dredge with flour. Cook gator in fat to brown. Add enough hot water to cover. Simmer

---

for 1 hour. Add carrots, shallots, corn, potatoes, onions, salt and pepper. Cook 30 minutes. Serve with rice. Great for Florida game.

> Ole timers in Athens will remember Leon Farmer's dad, Sarge, of the University ROTC. Leon likes life in the kitchen. He and his wife, Vickie, are avid fans of Georgia sports teams and enjoy cooking out. When Sarge got a Budweiser distributorship, Leon knew he would have a job after college. Today, he runs his distributorship so successfully that he, Vickie and his son, Leon, are major donors to Bulldog athletic teams.

Wedge's Old Fashioned Brunswick Stew

LEON & VICKIE FARMER

6 large chicken breasts
6-8 chicken thighs (depending on size)
3-4 pound beef roast
3-4 pound pork roast
5 cans Campbell's chicken broth
1 can Campbell's beef broth
1 cup chopped celery
1 cup chopped Vidalia onion
1/2 cup chopped carrots
2 tbs. finely minced garlic
2 bay leaves
Water

Boil 6 chicken breasts and 6 to 8 chicken thighs in 3 cans

continued

of Campbell's Chicken Broth and enough water to cover. Add ½ cup of chopped celery, ½ cup of chopped onions, ¼ cup of chopped carrots (all chopped medium-fine), 1 tablespoon of finely minced garlic, and 1 bay leaf to the cooking broth. Cook until done. Remove chicken and let cool. When cool, pull chicken meat from bone and chop into pieces. Discard bones and reserve chicken meat. Remove bay leaf from broth. Let broth cool and scoop off the fat that rises to the top. Reserve the broth and cooked vegetables.

Cut a small beef roast (3 to 4 pounds) into pieces (about an inch square), and cut a small pork roast (3-4 pounds) into pieces ab out the same size). Boil the beef and pork in a separate pot from the chicken in 2 cans of Campbell's Chicken Broth and 1 can of Campbell's Beef Broth and enough water to cover. Add ½ cup of chopped celery, ½ cup of chopped onions, ¼ cup of chopped carrots (all chopped medium-fine), 1 tablespoon of finely minced garlic, and 1 bay leaf and to the beef and pork broth. Let broth cool and scoop off the fat that rises to the top. Reserve the beef and pork broth and cooked vegetables.

Place some beef, pork, and chicken meat in Cuisinart, adding in a little broth from the chicken pot and a little broth from the beef and pork pot along with some of the cooked vegetables. Operate Cuisinart, chopping evenly until no large pieces remain. Pour from Cuisinart into a clean very large pot. Keep processing the beef, pork and chicken, chicken broth, beef and pork broth, and the cooked vegetables until all of the meat is uniformly chopped. You should have some broth left over. Reserve it for later to get the right consistency for the stew.

Add the following to the chopped meat and broth:

1 bag (16 oz) Green Giant white shoepeg corn
1 package (16 oz) John Cope's white cream corn (or other brand)
½ cup Heinz white vinegar
¼ cup Lea and Perrins Worcestershire sauce
1 tsp. poultry seasoning
¼ tsp. allspice
1 tsp. white pepper
1 tsp. black pepper
¼ tsp. red pepper
1 tsp. Hot sauce (Tabasco or Crystal-Tabasco is hotter)
3 cans (14½ oz. each) of Del Monte Fresh Cut Diced Tomatoes
2 cans (15 oz. each) tomato sauce
2 large Vidalia (or other sweet) onions chopped
1 stick butter
¼ cup brown sugar
Juice of 2 lemons
Juice of 1 lime
¼ cup Kraft Hickory Smoked Barbecue Sauce
Salt to taste (there is some salt in the broth)

Stir well and cook slowly for several hours. Don't let it stick to the pot or burn. Add remaining chicken broth and beef and pork broth as needed. If the stew is still too thick, add water as needed for the right consistency.

This is an old Farmer family recipe that was brought down from Virginia many years ago and recently modernized by Leon Farmer Jr., a descendent.

Vegetable Soup

THELMA ROBINSON, GEORGIA CENTER

5 lbs. ground beef
½ case diced potatoes
½ pan celery
2 bags English peas
2 bags mixed vegetables
1 quart chicken base
1 bag corn
½ case limas
1 case tomatoes, diced
1 case green beans
Water
Salt
Pepper

Note: Thelma prepares this soup at the Georgia Center everyday and this is the portion she makes for the day.

When Bob Poss died, I really hurt. We had been friends for years. We partied together, we traveled together and we laughed at endless stories and scenes from the Super Bowl to all the college football bowls Georgia played in. Possey, a reserve guard on the Rose Bowl team of '42, was famous for saying that ten years after graduation he made all-conference. Twenty years later he was All-American. "It won't be long," he would quip, "that I'll get the Heisman trophy."

Poss had a sterling career in the food business, principally with barbecue and hash. He manufactured it, he sold it and he was good at grilling and cooking. For years, one of the highlights of the preseason was the election of the football captains at his restaurant on the Atlanta Highway.

He loved to laugh, eat and party with his friends. He was fond of saying, "if you eat my product, you think about me all night."

"Bobby-Q" was one of his nicknames. He contributed to every cause in Athens, every sports team at Athens High and Georgia. He sold his barbecue at Sanford Stadium for years. He loved Georgia and its people. And when he left this earth it removed a big heart, the biggest, from the community. But up there in barbecue heaven, he has to be smiling that his son-in-law Mike Williams is carrying on the barbecue tradition at Pinecrest Lodge.

Poss Famous Hash

BETTY POSS

3 chicken fryers, cut up OR
6 lbs. chicken breast
3 lbs. beef chuck roast
3 lbs. Boston butt pork roast
3 baking potatoes, peeled
2 large onions
5 (14.5 oz.) can tomatoes, pureed
⅔ cup brown sugar
⅔ cup cider vinegar
½ cup ketchup

Combine chicken, beef and pork in large pot. Cover with water and cook until meat is almost done. About 30

continued

minutes before meat is done, add potatoes and onions and cook until meat is done and vegetables are tender. Drain, reserving stock. Remove meat from bones. Place meat, potatoes and onion in a food processor and blend. Return mixture to pot. Add pureed tomatoes, brown sugar, vinegar and ketchup. Bring to a simmer. Use reserved stock to thin as needed. Makes 7 to 8 quarts.

Seafood Jambalaya with Cheese Rice
STACY BANKSTON FIEDLER

½ cup bacon, cooked and chopped
1½ teaspoons roasted minced garlic
2 cups celery, chopped
1 large sweet onion (Vidalia works best), chopped
1 medium green bell pepper, chopped
½ cup olive oil
3 cans Hunts roasted garlic diced tomatoes
2 (6 oz.) cans Hunts tomato paste
1 cup water
1½ teaspoons sugar
2 teaspoons Worcestershire sauce
½ teaspoon hot pepper sauce
1 lb. smoked sausage, sliced
2 lbs. shrimp, peeled and de-veined
1 lb. sea scallops

In a large skillet, sauté bacon, garlic, celery, onion, and bell pepper in olive oil. Transfer to soup kettle. Add tomatoes, tomato paste, water, sugar, Worcestershire sauce, hot pepper sauce, salt and pepper. Bring to a boil. Reduce heat and simmer for 2½ hours. Cook shrimp

until they just turn pink and rinse off scallops. Add shrimp, scallops and sausage to the soup mixture. Simmer for an additional 30 minutes.

Rice
4 cups water
1 small sweet onion (Vidalia works best), chopped
2 cups yellow rice (Spanish flavor works best)
1 cup sharp cheddar cheese, shredded
2 teaspoons salt

Bring water to a boil. Stir in rice, onion and salt. Reduce heat, cover and simmer until done, approximately 20 minutes. Fold in cheese. Serve jambalaya over cheese rice.

Flowers Home Baked Chili
MACK & BETH LOWREY

2 medium onions, browned in bacon drippings
1½ lbs. ground beef, lightly browned
1½ teaspoons salt
½ teaspoon black pepper
¾ teaspoon chili powder
4 cans water
4 cans Campbell tomato soup
1 can (14 oz.) red kidney beans

Warm on top of stove, then bake at 350 degrees for 2 hours. Stir frequently to prevent sticking.

There is no player who was more colorful than Richard Appleby, an Athens native who grew up playing vacant lot football. Then he starred with Clarke Central and later with the Bulldogs, "a dream come true." If you are a fan of Georgia football, and you know Red and Black history, then you have to recall that game in Jacksonville when Florida led 7-3 in the fourth quarter. The late Bill Pace, who always had a special play in his offensive repertoire, designed the end around pass with Appleby taking a handoff from the quarterback and throwing deep to Gene Washington when the defense moved up for the end around. No defense ever bit harder than Florida's on November 8, 1975 in the old Gator Bowl. The 80-yard touchdown will long be remembered and so will Appleby's immortal words afterwards.

Following the game, I recorded a conversation with him and asked if he were nervous? He grinned and said, "You can say I was a little bit nervous, but you can say, I rose to the occasion."

Portuguese Bean Soup
RICHARD & JANE APPLEBY

Ham hocks or thick ham slices, diced
Portuguese sausage (1 hot and 1 mild), casing removed
   and sausage fried and fat drained off
1 can black bean soup, 2 cans water
1 can stewed tomatoes
1 small can lima beans
1 large can small red beans
1 large can green beans

cabbage, cut up
potatoes, optional
1 large can garbanzos
1 large can diced or sliced carrots
1 small can corn
1 large can white onions, cut up

Save the juice from the carrots and onions and add to soup. Simmer for several hours and serve.

Poor Stephens Chili
GREEK GEORGE

2 lbs. ground beef
2 (28 oz.) cans diced tomatoes
3 (14 oz.) cans Bush's chili beans
1 large chopped bell pepper
1 large chopped yellow onion
4 tablespoons ketchup
4 tablespoons chili powder
2 tablespoons cumin
3 tablespoons garlic
1 teaspoon oregano
1 teaspoon salt, 1 teaspoon pepper
Red cayenne pepper

Pour tomatoes and ketchup into a pot over medium heat. In a separate pot, sauté peppers and onions until soft, then add to pot with tomatoes. Sauté meat with 1 teaspoon garlic, drain, and add to pot with tomatoes and peppers. Add chili powder, cumin, garlic, oregano, salt and pepper. Let simmer for 1 hour. Add beans and simmer another $1/2$ hour. Add cayenne pepper to taste.

In the late seventies, I went home to Wrightsville to speak to the high school athletic banquet. A long time friend, Ralph Jackson, and I sat together. He pointed across the room to a sturdy young athlete and began to talk enthusiastically about him as a football player.

"His name is Herschel Walker," Ralph said, "and you should tell Coach Dooley about him. He is going to be something special."

At the time, as I recall, Herschel was in the tenth grade. So I did as I always do. I returned home and told the coaches which brought about a good bit of needling. "Y'all have football down there?" they chided me. But the next spring when Herschel ran :09.7 in a track meet, the chiding stopped. Coaches began to flock to my little hometown. And you know the rest of the story.

It was great fun having Herschel on campus, winning games and championships. He made many long runs and pounded away for countless first downs, but I'll always consider his performance in the Sugar Bowl for the national championship the one I remember best.

His shoulder was dislocated on the first offensive play from scrimmage. Usually that injury will sideline a back indefinitely but Herschel went back into the game and took 35 snaps right into the teeth of that Notre Dame defense, a defense that did not give up a hundred yards rushing to any single player all season. Notre Dame was determined to deny Herschel. He gained 150 yards on the afternoon.

I still have some of the poetry he wrote for the book, "Glory, Glory." When I see Herschel today, I see the same Herschel of 1980. Broad shoulders, small waistline and dancing hips. Svelte and sleek he will always be.

Lentil Soup

CINDY & HERSCHEL WALKER

2 cloves garlic
1 onion
1 celery stick
2 carrots
1 bag of lentils
1 or 2 smoked hamhocks
1 bundle of kale or escarole
olive oil

Process onions, garlic, celery and carrots in a food processor. Sauté all in olive oil. (Enough olive oil to cover the bottom of the pan.) rinse lentils and add them to the sautéed mixture with about a half gallon of water. Add hamhock and simmer till done. Add salt and pepper to taste. Will require simmering for approximately two hours or so.

Michelle Clovis has been a sorority housemother at Georgia for many years. She loves the Dogs and she prepares for a special menu each Friday, based on the mascots of the team which is next on the schedule.

South Carolina is easy. That is when chicken is prepared. Florida is easy too. She has gator tails shipped up for frying just like chicken fingers. For Tennessee it is "smoky" ribs. Low country boil or etoufee for LSU. Barbecue pig for Arkansas. In lieu of Tiger meat for Auburn, she often prepares Brunswick stew. Since Auburn is referred to as the

War Eagles, sometimes turkey can be served. What about the Commodores of Vandy, the Yellow Jackets of Georgia Tech or the Crimson Tide of Alabama?

"Those are a little more difficult," she says. "What we do in those cases is get revved up for the game with a variety of hotdogs — slaw dogs, chili dogs and corndogs".

LSU Okra Gumbo

MICHELE CLOVIS

16 oz. frozen okra (cut, cooked and drained)
3 tsp. butter
1 cup finely chopped green onions
1 medium bell pepper (red) chopped
1/2 cup parsley chopped
2 cloves minced garlic
16 oz. stew tomatoes
16 oz. tomato sauce
11 oz. condensed chicken bouillon
Cayenne pepper
Thyme
Oregano
Basil
Tabasco sauce
Worcestershire sauce
Bay leaves
3 cups cooked chicken (diced)
1 cup chopped ham (diced and cooked)

In 6 quart pan melt butter, add onions, bell peppers, parsley, garlic. Sauté until softened. Add tomatoes and tomato sauce and chicken bouillon. Bring to a boil. Reduce heat and add seasonings, chicken, okra and ham. Simmer 40 minutes. Serve with/over rice.

Bulldog Chili

RON & EILEEN COURSON

4 tablespoons vegetable oil
2 large onions, chopped
3 bell peppers, chopped
1 pound lean ground beef
2 tablespoons chili powder
Crushed red pepper (to taste)
Cayenne pepper (to taste)
1 tablespoon salt
1/2 teaspoon black pepper
1 (16 oz.) can of tomatoes
2 (16 oz.) kidney beans

Combine the vegetable oil, onions and bell pepper in a deep pot. Cook slowly for 20 minutes with cover on. Brown ground beef in a skillet and drain. Add browned ground beef to onions and bell peppers along with the rest of the ingredients and cook slowly for 1 hour. Chili is spicy and hot. Adjust seasonings if a milder chili is desired.

Sonny Perdue was a walk on football player for the Bulldogs. He pulled off a stunning political upset in November as everybody in Georgia knows.

He'll be following the Dogs with great interest as chief executive of the state of Georgia. He spoke to the team in November after being elected and enjoys recalling his days as a walk on football player.

I suspect he enjoys tailgating as much as anybody. He has a wide and generous smile, which suggests that he is an advocate of good food and warm fellowship. I know he'll be tailgating often with Dog fans in the days ahead.

Crab Chowder

SONNY & MARY PERDUE

¼ teaspoon minced garlic
⅛ teaspoon cayenne
¼ cup green pepper
1 tablespoon butter
2 cans potato soup
1 package cream cheese
1 ½ cans milk
6 ounces crabmeat
1 can whole kernel corn
Chopped onions
⅛ cup sugar

Cook onions, garlic, peppers, and cayenne in butter. Blend in soup, cream cheese, and milk. Add crabmeat. Add undrained corn; bring to a boil. Reduce heat and simmer for 10 minutes. Stir in sugar.

SALADS

Happy to meet the Bear after the flea flicker.

When Tubby Smith got the basketball job at Georgia, many expected a rotund, heavy, big girthed man to show up. It didn't take long for everyone to learn that there was nothing heavy about Tubby, who got his name when he was growing up in the Chesapeake Bay area. He is lean and svelte. And mean on the basketball court.

Life was austere for Tubby's family of 17 children. His daddy had a plethora of jobs to make ends meet. Everything was a make do existence. Baths were taken in an old washtub, and every one of the kids had a turn. When it became Tubby's turn, he enjoyed sloshing around in the water so much that he wouldn't get out. That is why his mother nick-named him Tubby. It stuck.

And when it came to mealtime, Tubby's mother knew what foods to prepare. Food that working class people know you have to have. Food that sticks to your ribs.

When he was coaching at Georgia, I coaxed him into taking me up to Scotland, Md. to meet his mother and dad. It was a wonderful trip and left me inspired with what I saw and learned. It doesn't matter how tough life is, if you want to survive and succeed, you can do it. It takes parental discipline, leadership and hard work.

It is sad that we seem to have lost parental motivation and discipline. Sad, too, that the work ethic is not being underscored. Discipline and the work ethic enabled Tubby Smith to succeed in life and he and Donna will always be an inspiration for Myrna and me.

Zesty Seafood Salad
DONNA & TUBBY SMITH

1 cup mayonnaise
2 tbsp. French dressing
½ cup chili sauce
1 tbsp. lemon juice
1 tbsp. capers (optional)
2 tsp. Horseradish
½ tsp. Worcestershire sauce
1 tsp. Seasoning salt
Pinch of pepper
Approx. 1-2 tsp. Bay Food Seasoning
Approx. 1 tsp. Red pepper to taste
1½ lb. Shrimp cooked shelled and deveined,
    cut into bite size pieces
1 lb. Crabmeat or more to taste (use backfin crabmeat)
1 tbsp. dry minced onion
¾ tsp. salt

Combine all ingredients except shrimp and crabmeat. Stir well. Pour over mixed shrimp and crabmeat and stir lightly. Cover and chill 2 to 3 hours. Serve on lettuce and garnished tomato wedges. Provides 6 to 8 portions.

Earl Leonard, a colorful character and a serious student of political history, especially that of his home state, worked as the late Senator Richard B. Russell's press secretary. I visited with him often in Washington and he encouraged me to take a similar job with Rep. Phil Landrum, one of the most powerful men in the House of Representatives. Myrna and

I were planning to be married, and I wasn't sure about finding her a job in the D.C. area, so I opted for a job at the Georgia Center on campus.

One day sitting with Earl in Sen. Russell's office, he told me he was leaving Georgia's senior senator and returning to Atlanta to work for Coca Cola. He managed his stock options and splits into a nice fortune. I was bragging on Earl one day, rather excessively which caused a listener to ask, "Why are you all such good friends?"

This was my reply. "He has a big expense account, he has a house in the mountains and a house at Ponte Vedra. Why wouldn't you be friends with somebody like that?"

Wild Rice Chicken Salad

BEBE & EARL LEONARD

2 (6.2 oz.) packages long-grain and wild rice mix
2 (6 oz.) jars marinated artichoke quarters, undrained
4 cups chopped cooked chicken
1 medium size red bell pepper, chopped
2 celery ribs, thinly sliced
5 green onions, chopped
1 (2.25 oz.) can sliced ripe olives, drained
1 cup mayonnaise
1 1/2 teaspoons curry powder
Leaf lettuce

Cook rice mix according to package directions. Drain artichoke quarters, reserving 1/2 cup liquid. Stir together rice, artichoke, chicken and next 4 ingredients. Stir together artichoke liquid, mayonnaise and curry powder. Toss with rice mixture. Cover and chill 8 hours. Serve on leaf lettuce. Make 8 servings. Recipe can be made without the chicken.

Tortellini Salad

KELLY & TOM JOHNSON

1 (8 oz.) package cheese tortellini
1 tomato, diced
1 cup olives, sliced
Broccoli, steamed and chopped
Hearts of palm, chopped
1 tablespoon Dijon mustard
4 tablespoons red wine vinegar
1 teaspoon sugar
1/2 teaspoon salt
1/2 teaspoon pepper
1/2 cup olive oil
Freshly grated parmesan cheese

Cook cheese tortellini according to directions, drain and put in serving bowl. Add tomatoes, broccoli, olives and hearts of palm. Set aside. In a separate container, mix mustard, vinegar, sugar, salt and pepper. Blend with a wire whisk. Add olive oil. Continue to whisk as it is added. Pour dressing over salad and gently toss. Add parmesan to taste.

South of the Border Cornbread Salad

ALLENE MASSEY

1 pan cornbread, crumbled
2 cups shredded lettuce
1 cup chopped bell pepper
3 large tomatoes, chopped
2 (16 oz.) cans pinto beans, drained
2 (16 oz.) cans whole kernel corn, drained
1 cup sliced green onions
1 (16 oz) bottle ranch dressing
1 (8 oz.) package shredded cheddar cheese
10 slices crisp cooked bacon, crumbled

Layer half the ingredients in a dish in the order given. Repeat layers. Makes 8 servings.

Halls of Fame often bring about a lot of injustices. None greater than in the case of Georgia's John Rauch. Best we can tell John is the only player in NCAA history to start every game for four years plus four bowl games.

John belongs in the College Football Hall of Fame. I talked to two coaches who worked with him when John was head coach of the Oakland Raiders and played in the Super Bowl. They had plenty to say about John Rauch and his creativity when it came to offensive football. Their names: Bill Walsh and John Madden.

All of us at Georgia are still working to promote John's election into the Hall. This deserving man is, perhaps, the most modest of all those who were as

successful as a player and coach as he was.

I told him once that he unquestionably deserved membership in the College Football Hall of Fame. At the time his coach, Wallace Butts, had not been admitted, and John said: "Don't worry about me. I'll be satisfied if Coach Butts gets in."

You could say John is satisfied now since Coach Butts was elected in 1997. But those of us on the Bulldog athletic staff are not satisfied...and won't be until John Rauch is elected.

Linguine Salad

JOHN & JANE RAUCH

1 medium zucchini, thinly sliced
½ cup julienned carrots
½ cup fresh or frozen pea pods
3 cups cooked linguine
¾ cup julienne sweet red pepper

Dressing

3 tbs. white wine vinegar or cider vinegar
2 tbs. olive or canola oil
2 tsp. Dijon mustard
1 clove garlic, minced
1 tsp. sugar
1 tsp. dried thyme, optional
½ tsp. salt
¼ tsp. white pepper

Place zucchini and carrots in a steamer basket; place in saucepan over 1 inch of boiling water. Cover and steam

continued

for 2 to 3 minutes. Add pea pods; steam for 1 minute longer. Transfer vegetables to a large bowl; add cooked linguine and red pepper.

In small bowl whisk together the dressing ingredients. Pour over linguine mixture and toss to coat. Cover and refrigerate for 1 hour or until serving. Serves 4.

Seven Layered Salad

JENNIFER BROWN

Layer chopped lettuce
Layer English peas
Layer cooked chopped bacon
Layer sliced boiled eggs (sprinkle with salt and pepper)
Layer tomato (diced)
Layer grated cheddar cheese

Great in a large casserole dish.

Seven Layer Salad

MICHELE CLOVIS

1 head lettuce (torn)
1 cup chopped celery
1 cup chopped green pepper
1 cup onion rings (thinly sliced)
1 pkg. Frozen green peas (cooked, cooled and drained)
1½ cup mayonnaise
Parmesan cheese
Bacon crumbs

Cover bottom of 9" x 12" Pyrex dish with torn lettuce and put next 4 ingredients on top of lettuce in layers. Put mayonnaise on top layer. Sprinkle parmesan cheese and bacon on top. Refrigerate for 8 hours, covered really well.

Vegetable Salad

JOHN & JANE RAUCH

1 can angle cut green beans
1 can Lesueur peas
1 can shoepeg corn
1 small jar chopped pimentos
4 ribs celery chopped
1 purple onion chopped
1 green pepper chopped

Heat 1 tsp. Salt, ¾ cups sugar, ¾ cups oil, ½ cup vinegar, ¼ tsp. water to dissolve sugar. Pour over vegetables. Marinate overnight. Keeps well. Serves 12.

Athens mayor Doc Eldridge grew up in Athens, played football for Weyman Sellers at Athens High which became Clarke Central. His favorite Georgia memory came when he was playing, with friends, on the hillside at the Northwest corner of Sanford Stadium. The kids who gathered there didn't always watch the game, but in the '65 game with Alabama and Georgia backed up inside the Bulldog thirty yard line, the kids all quit tussling and wrestling and decided to watch the game. Good timing, for they feasted their eyes on one of the greatest plays in Bulldog history. After the snap, Kirby Moore passed to Pat Hodgson who lateralled to Bob Taylor for a 73-yard touchdown, which led to victory.

"I'll never forget that moment," Doc says. There have been many thrilling surprises like that throughout the years including the shoestring play against Vandy, a play designed by his father-in-law, the late Bill Pace.

Potato Salad

SHERI & DOC ELDRIDGE

8 medium potatoes, boiled in jackets
1½ cup mayonnaise
1 cup sour cream
1½ teaspoon horseradish
1 teaspoon celery seed
½ teaspoon salt
1 cup chopped fresh parsley
2 medium onions, finely minced

Peel potatoes and cut into ⅛" slices. Combine mayonnaise, sour cream, horseradish, celery seed and salt; set aside. In another bowl mix parsley and onions.

In a large serving bowl, arrange a layer of potatoes; salt lightly. Cover with a layer of mayonnaise/sour cream mixture, then a layer of the onion mixture. Continue layers ending with parsley and onion. DO NOT STIR! Cover and refrigerate at least 8 hours. It is better if made the day before. Makes 8 servings.

Iron Skillet Chicken Salad with Tarragon

TRICIA & JOHN BOSTWICK

4 chicken breasts
2 to 3 tablespoons olive oil
⅓ cup diced onions
⅓ cup diced celery
⅓ cup Dukes mayonnaise
½ tablespoon dried tarragon
⅛ tablespoon celery salt
1 hard boiled egg, chopped
salt and pepper to taste

Preheat oven to 400 degrees.

Sprinkle breasts with salt and pepper. Add the olive oil to a cast iron skillet and put over high heat. Sear the chicken breasts on both sides for about 2 minutes on each side. Place iron skillet in oven for 8 to 10 minutes. Remove the breasts and let cool until you can handle them. Tear breast apart into small pieces, then lightly chop them. Add all of the onions, celery, tarragon, celery salt and chopped egg. Then blend with Dukes mayonnaise.

Hunker Down Hairy Dawg Potato Salad

LYDIA & CURTIS MCGILL

10 lbs. "Red" new potatoes
8 hard boiled eggs
1 medium jar sweet diced pickles
½ cup diced celery
2 tbs. onion flakes
½ cups "Blue Plate" mayonnaise
½ cup mustard
Salt to taste

Peel, cube and cook potatoes until tender. Drain and cool potatoes. Boil eggs and dice. Mix potatoes, eggs, celery, onion flakes, pickles, salt, mayonnaise and mustard. Potato salad mixture should be a little soupy. Potato salad will soak up mayonnaise and mustard and will taste better if prepared the day before being served. Prepare on Friday for tailgate on Saturday! Potato salad is and has been a must for all Saturday "Dawn Tailgates" for the McGills! Serves 20.

Layered BLT Salad

ANDREA & JOHN WITHERS

1 (8 oz.) container sour cream
1 cup mayonnaise
1 tablespoon lemon juice
1 teaspoon dried basil
½ teaspoon salt
½ teaspoon pepper
¼ teaspoon garlic powder

1 large head iceberg lettuce, torn, about 4 cups, may also use red leaf lettuce
1 (32 oz.) package thick bacon slices, cooked and crumbled
6 plum tomatoes, thinly sliced
3 cups large croutons

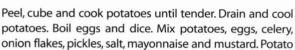

Stir together first 7 ingredients until well blended.

Layer lettuce, bacon and tomato in a 13" x 9" baking dish. Spread mayonnaise mixture evenly over tomato, sealing to edge of dish. Cover and chill salad at least 2 hours. Sprinkle with croutons and serve immediately. Makes 8 servings.

Curried Chicken Salad

KAREN & JIM HOLBROOK

4 cups cold chicken breast, cut into cubes (about 4 large breast, cooked)
2 green onions, including tops, sliced thin and diced
¼ cup white raisins, steamed
¾ cup green grapes, split
½ cup roasted sliced almonds
2 tablespoons lime or lemon juice
½ teaspoon grated lemon rind
½ to ¾ cup mayonnaise
2 teaspoons crystallized ginger, finely chopped
½ to 1 teaspoon curry powder (or more to taste)
2 to 4 tablespoons mango chutney (or more to taste)
1 cup sliced and diced Granny Smith apple with lemon juice poured over it to prevent darkening
⅔ cup sliced celery

Out of the blue one day, Jack Nicklaus called me and said that his daughter, Nan, was interested in Georgia. She was a good volleyball player and wound up enrolling in Athens to play volleyball. She and Myrna spent a lot of time together. Nan was often at our house, washing her clothes, grabbing a beer from the fridge and getting to know our kids, Camille and Kent.

We had plenty of parties for the young folks at our house. I told Jack when Nan and her husband-to-be, Bill O'Leary, Bulldog tight end, graduated, I was looking for some time off from partying.

Today the O'Learys have five children, four boys and a girl. If there is anything Jack likes as much as major championships, it is grandchildren. My hope is that their genes are handed down and that one day, one of them will wear a Bulldog football uniform.

Hot Chicken Salad

BILL & NAN O'LEARY

3 cups cooked chicken breast
1 cup slivered almonds
1 can water chestnuts (sliced)
1 small red pimento (drained)
2 cups celery
1 tsp. salt
½ tsp. pepper
1 tbsp. lemon juice
1½ cups Hellman's Mayonnaise
1 cup cheese
1 can cream of chicken soup
1 can onion rings

Bake 45 minutes at 325 degrees in a 13" x 9" baking dish. Onions last 10 minutes. Remove from oven and let stand approximately 10 minutes before cutting into squares and serving.

24 – Hour Summer (or Fall) Salad

TINA & NEIL WILLIAMSON
Neil is with WSB and is the co-host of the Tailgate Show

2 heads iceberg lettuce
1 medium Vidalia onion
1 red bell pepper
1 package frozen peas, thawed but not cooked
1 (8 oz,) package shredded cheddar cheese
6 strips bacon
Parmesan cheese
2 cups mayonnaise
3 tablespoons sugar

Tear lettuce into small pieces and arrange in bottom of glass bowl. Chop Vidalia onion and arrange atop lettuce. Chop bell pepper and sprinkle atop the onion. Spread peas evenly over onion and bell pepper.

In a separate container, mix 2 cups mayonnaise with 3 tablespoons sugar. Spread mixture atop the pea layer in bowl. Sprinkle cheddar cheese layer over mayonnaise so that it covers to edges. Continue with a crumbled bacon layer. Sprinkle with parmesan cheese just before serving.

Cover glass bowl with plastic wrap, tightly securing all edges. Refrigerate for 24 hours.

Makes 6 to 8 servings.

Cornbread Salad

GOVERNOR ROY & MARIE BARNES

Self rising cornmeal mix
1 cup sour cream
2 eggs

Mix and bake at 450 degrees until done. While it cools, cut up 1 each: Onions, tomatoes, sweet pickles and bell peppers. Mix with cornbread and 1 cup mayonnaise. Chill. Make previous night and refrigerate.

Fami Slaw

BETH BERNARD

1 head cabbage, chopped
8 tablespoons sesame seeds
8 tablespoons almonds
2 packages ramen noodles
8 green onions

Brown almonds and sesame seeds in butter. Mix cabbage and onion in large bowl. At last minute, add sesame seeds, almonds and crushed raw ramen noodles. Pour dressing over immediately before serving.

Dressing

4 tablespoons sugar
1 cup salad oil
6 tablespoons red wine vinegar
1 tablespoons pepper
2 tablespoons salt

Greek Pasta Salad

FRANK & MARY BETH CRUMLEY

4 boneless breasts of chicken (optional)
Greek all purpose seasoning
1 (8 oz.) Paul Newman's Own olive oil and vinegar
  dressing
1 (4 oz.) feta cheese
1 (16 oz.) tri-color corkscrew pasta
black olives (optional)

Cut up boneless breast of chicken into cubes and sprinkle with Greek seasoning. In a large frying pan cook chicken. Add additional seasoning if needed. Boil water and cook pasta. Transfer pasta to large bowl. Add chicken and Newman's Own dressing to pasta. You may not need the entire bottle, pour to your taste. Add feta cheese and sprinkle Greek seasoning for taste. Toss ingredients. Garnish with black olives (Optional). Can be served hot or at room temperature.

There have been many times when Georgia was riding high, that after one of Kid Terrell's tailgate parties that many of us showed up at Terry and Joy Wingfield's house.

Mainly because Terry wanted to keep the party going and because he makes the best "Heavenly Tiddlies" in town.

For many years, we kidded him that he saw more sunrises than he did sunsets, but it wasn't because he was an early riser. Many of us, even today, like to party with Terry whose other favorite drink is a

Ellie's Coleslaw

JOHN & ELINOR TERRELL

1 head cabbage
2 tbsp. Sugar
¼ cup tarragon vinegar
¼ cup sweet pickle relish
1 grated carrot (optional)
½ cup Marzetti slaw dressing
½ to ¾ cup mayonnaise
Salt and pepper to taste

Shred cabbage as fine as possible. Add other ingredients and mix well. Better if refrigerated for several hours. Serves 10 to 12 people.

24-Hour Slaw

BUNNY & CLISBY CLARKE

1 head of cabbage, knife shredded
2 small onions, thinly sliced
1 cup white vinegar
½ cup sugar
1 tablespoon yellow mustard
1 tablespoon celery seed
1 tablespoon salt
¾ cup salad oil (canola or olive)
Pepper to taste

Layer cabbage and onion in a large bowl and sprinkle over mixture. Do not stir. Combine the vinegar, mustard, celery seed, salt and pepper. Boil ingredients for 1 minute, then add the oil. Bring to a boil again and pour over cabbage and onion. Do not stir. Best if allow to marinate for 24 hours. Serves 8. Keeps for about 2 weeks.

Chicken Broccoli Slaw

ANNE & JIM MINTER

2 chicken breasts cooked and chopped
1 pkg. prepared broccoli slaw
½ cup sunflower kernels
½ cup toasted slivered almonds
½ cup pine nuts
2 cans mandarin oranges drained (8 oz cans)
2 green onions
2 pkg. Ramen Chicken Noodles crushed before adding

continued

Mix all of the above ingredients, then add dressing.

Dressing

2 pkg flavoring (from noodle package)
½ cup sugar
½ cup Canola Oil
½ cup red wine vinegar

Pour over slaw mix before serving. Serves 10.

BREADS

Over the top — Herschel always soared at the goal line.

him. He jumped on a table and led a resounding cheer:
DAMN GOOD TEAM!
DAMN GOOD TEAM!

"If Dooley is reserved with his players, Erskine Russell more than fills the gap between the coaches and the players. He's a man's man, if that archaic phrase still stands in these times. Erk won't let you down. You know that. That is why so many of those who have played for him have played so hard for him on Saturday afternoons."

Erk Russell meant a lot to the Georgia football program. His unbridled enthusiasm was spontaneous and electrified locker rooms. He always had a quip for any occasion. He could say an uplifting word for any circumstance.

When Lewis Grizzard and I wrote "Glory, Glory" in 1981 here were my thoughts on Erk.

"He burst through the practice gates that first time in '64, assembled his first Georgia defense, looked them in their eyes and said, "You're good enough to play for me and you're good enough to win."

"Win they did. Seven games and an incredible second-place finish in the Southeastern Conference. The Florida game was something that year, Florida was supposed to cream Georgia.

"Late in the game, the score tied, 7-7, Bobby Etter, 140-pound kicker, lined up for a Georgia field goal attempt. There was a bad snap. Etter picked up the ball and ran it in for the touchdown. Georgia won, 14-7.

"The locker room in Jacksonville's Gator Bowl was bedlam. President O.C. Aderhold was hugging Dooley, players were screaming. Erk's emotion got the best of

Crispy Cheese Wafers
JEAN & ERK RUSSELL

1 cup butter
2 cups extra charp cheese
2 cups flour
½ tsp. Cayenne pepper
2 cups Rice Krispies
½ cup pecans (chopped)

Combine butter and cheese. Sift flour, salt and red pepper. Blend into butter and cheese mixture. Stir in cereal and nuts. Roll dough into small balls (size of marbles). Flatten with a fork. Bake at 350 degrees for 11 minutes or until lightly browned. You can make a long roll and slice them off and then mash with a fork (quicker). This didn't originate with me, but they are easy to make and can be kept for a good while.

Makes 10 dozen.

Zucchini Bread

PAIGE & TALLEY LAMBERT

3 eggs
1 cup salad oil
2 cups dark brown sugar, packed
2 cups grated raw unpeeled zucchini
3 cups all purpose flour
1 teaspoon salt
1 teaspoon baking soda
1 tablespoon vanilla
1 cup chopped nuts

Beat eggs, add oil, sugar and zucchini and mix. Stir in flour, which has been sifted together with salt and baking soda. Fold in vanilla and nuts. Pour into 2 greased, floured loaf pans (9" x 5" x 3"). Bake at 350 degrees for 1 hour.

Remove from pans and cool on a rack. Extra loaf freezes well.

Sausage Pinwheels

MARY ANN ROBERTS

Mary Ann Roberts is married to former Georgia player and coach, Jack Roberts

2 cans crescent rolls
1 package Bruce Williams sausage

Put sausage on rolls, need not separate. Roll long way and put in freezer or refrigerator for 3 hours or so. Slice and bake at 350 degrees for 15 to 20 minutes. Real good warm.

Stew's Famous Swiss Cheese and Pickle on Rye

STEWART S. RICHARDSON, JR.

Kraft Swiss cheese
Clausen's refrigerated sandwich sliced dill pickles
Hellmann's mayonnaise
Gulden's yellow mustard
Pepperidge Farm, Arnold's or any high quality sliced
    loaf rye bread

It is a simple sandwich but with a crispy distinct flavor that tailgaters love, but they must be made correctly!

So that the sandwiches remain fresh for several hours, generously put mayonnaise and mustard on each of the 2 slices of bread. Then, cut the already sliced Swiss cheese to fit the slices of bread without going over the edges and place on bread.

Using specifically Clausen sandwich sliced pickles, place the sliced pickles on top of the cheese, each side by side in order to cover the entire slice of cheese. You will find that some of the sliced pickles are longer. Place the longer pickles in the middle of the cheese and the shorter pickles toward the outside so as to fit the contour of the loaf of bread. As needed, cut off the ends of the pickles so as to fit the slice of bread with the cheese. You don't want the ends of the pickles stickling out from the bread.

Put either the piece of bread with the mayo or mustard on top. Then, with a large knife, cut the sandwiches into four squares to make finger sandwiches. Cut the ends of the bread off first-only if you like. Then store in a Tupperware container and keep chilled in a cooler until ready to serve. You will see that your fellow tailgaters will gravitate toward these simple but tasty sandwiches.

Whispering Bill Anderson, has a journalism degree from Georgia, and often calls me in the Fall to see what is going on with the Dogs. With an enthusiastic and generous laugh, Bill loves a good joke and a good story. He returns to Commerce every year to put on a country music benefit for local charities.

Although he grew up in Decatur, Commerce is an adopted hometown. If you listen to the words of his song, "City Lights" which brought him unlimited financial success, you would think Bill got the inspiration by looking out of a tall hotel in some big city, like Chicago, from the 75th floor looking down on the lights of the street. Not so.

One summer when he was working at WJJC he went home one night and from the roof of the old Andrew Jackson Hotel he looked down to the streetlights of downtown Commerce and composed that award winning song.

Shortbread Squares
BILL ANDERSON

1 cup butter, softened
1 cup packed light brown sugar
1 egg yolk
1 teaspoon vanilla
2 cups all-purpose flour
¼ teaspoon salt
4 Hershey (regular size) milk chocolate candy bars, broken into pieces
¾ cup pecans, chopped

In mixing bowl, cream together butter and brown sugar. Add egg yolk and vanilla. Mix well.

Sift together flour and salt. Add to creamed mixture. Press into greased 15" x 10" baking pan. Bake at 350 degrees for 15 to 18 minutes till golden brown.

Remove from oven and immediately place candy bar pieces on top of baked crust. Let sit till candy melts. Then spread chocolate evenly over crust and sprinkle with nuts. Cool. Cut into squares.

Monkey Bread
RUBY & HAROLD HODGSON, JR.

4 tubes of 10 biscuits
1 cup sugar
1 teaspoon cinnamon
1½ sticks margarine
1¼ cup brown sugar
½ cup chopped nuts

Cut biscuits in 4 pieces. Roll each piece in 1 cup sugar and 1 teaspoon cinnamon combined. Drop into heavily greased Bundt pan. When all pieces have been coated, sprinkle remaining mixture over biscuits.

Melt and combine margarine, brown sugar and 1½ teaspoons cinnamon. Add nuts and pour over top of biscuits.

Bake at 325 degrees for 45 minutes. Cool 5 minutes. Remove from pan.

Sausage Balls

JENNIFER BROWN

1 lb. hot sausage
1 lb. sharp cheese, grated
2 ½ cups Bisquick

Mix all ingredients together and roll into small balls 1" diameter. Place on cookie sheet. Bake at 350 degrees until brown. Great snack!

Pecan Cheesies

NANCY & AL THOMPSON

Nancy is the youngest of Coach Wallace Butts' three daughters.
She was a cheerleader at Georgia.

¾ lbs. New York Sharp cheese, grated
2 sticks butter or margarine (at room temperature)
3 cups all purpose flour
⅛ tsp. Red pepper or paprika (optional)
1 tsp. Salt
Pecan halves

Cream butter and cheese. Add flour and salt gradually. Make into three equal balls and then into cylindrical rolls. Wrap each role in paper towels. Refrigerate several hours. Slick into ¼" thick rounds. Top with pecan halves. Bake at 375 degrees for 10 to 15 minutes.

Our friend Dave Robertson of Toronto is without question the most unusual Georgia football fan. You can underscore unusual. He lives in Toronto, a Canadian who is a Georgia graduate. What is so unusual about Dave? He sees at least half of Georgia's games every year. And get this, he drives to Athens when he wants to see the 'Dogs play. You heard right. He drives. I know for I flew to Toronto late one Thanksgiving afternoon. Spent the night with him and we motored to Atlanta on Friday for a game with Georgia Tech.

He has been following this routine for years. In recent times, however, he has not headed South as much as he once did since his son, Michael, is an outstanding hockey player and has had a busy schedule of games.

"I always get there for one or two games even though television covers so many games," Dave says. "I'd still rather see the Bulldogs in living color between the hedges. Nothing like being a Dog fan. When it is in your blood, it is there forever."

Crescent Cups

DAVE & DIANNE ROBERTSON

In a small bowl combine:
1 cup chopped ham or chicken
2 chopped hard-boiled eggs
1 cup shredded cheddar cheese
⅓ cup chopped celery
⅓ cup frozen peas
¼ cup Miracle Whip
Pinch of dry mustard

Take one tube of Pillsbury crescent roll dough and separate the crescents. Re-shape into shells in a muffin tray. Spoon the mixture into the cups. Bake at 375 degrees for 10 to 15 minutes.

Great hot or cold. Makes eight crescent cups.

You can also use tart shells if you wish. Cook slightly longer until golden brown.

Sausage-Cheese Balls

MARY ANN ROBERTS

1 pound Bruce Williams sausage
2 cups Bisquick mix
1 cup sharp cheese, grated

Mix all ingredients in a bowl. The moisture in the sausage will be enough to moisten the Bisquick. Roll mixture into balls the size of a walnut. Bake at 350 degrees for 15 to 20 minutes.

After the '59 Georgia-Auburn game in Athens, you know, the Tarkenton to Herron sensational game winning score, it has always been strange to see Pat Dye on the War Eagle sideline. (Guess the Auburn people felt the same way about Vince.) Pat, you recall recovered the fumble that set up the winning TD pass.

I have always maintained a close friendship with Pat, a devotee of the outdoors. We talk hunting and fishing from time to time, and, of course, football.

Pat is a remarkable conversationalist, especially when it comes to football. He is knowledgeable, loves the game and if he has time to talk, very patient with anyone listening.

Once I went over to his farm and he gave me a tour on a wet, chilly day. As the mud flew off the tires of his four-wheeler onto my windbreaker, he reminisced about his days in Athens. No player ever loved his coach more than Pat Dye loved Wallace Butts.

Even today, if you bring up Butts' name you can see his eyes twinkle and moist up.

Pat is an advocate of the view when it comes to hunting and fishing that you need to eat what you kill. His freezer usually is stocked full of fish and quail, dove and deer. And turkey.

He can cook too, and if he invites you for a meal, be sure and accept his invitation.

Cheese Wafers

COACH PAT DYE

2 cups butter or margarine, softened
4 cups all purpose flour
1 to 2 tsp. ground red pepper
1 pound block sharp Cheddar cheese, shredded
½ tsp. salt
½ tsp. paprika

Beat butter and shredded cheese at medium speed with an electric mixer until blended; add flour and remaining ingredients, beating until blended. Cover dough and chill

continued

2 hours. Shape dough into 4 (8-inch) logs; cover and chill 8 hours. Cut into ¼ inch slices, and place on ungreased baking sheets. Bake at 350 degrees for 15 minutes. Remove to wire racks to cool. Store in an airtight container. (These keep well in an airtight container and are good with salad or as appetizer). Makes 10 dozen.

Beer Muffins
KATHERINE CLARKE

3 cups Bisquick
½ cup sugar
1 (12 oz.) can beer

Mix and bake in hot greased muffin tins, ⅔ full, at 400 degrees until light golden-brown on top. Baking time may vary due to oven temperature. Test with toothpick after 8 to 10 minutes. Makes about 2 dozen.

Cheesecrackers
SANDRA & BEN BELUE

1 lb. grated sharp cheese
1 cup butter (2 sticks)
3 cups plain flour, sifted
1 teaspoon salt
½ teaspoon red pepper
½ cup finely chopped pecans

Leave cheese and butter out the night before to soften. Mix all ingredients working with your hands. Shape into

four rolls and roll in waxed paper. Refrigerate until firm and slice thin. Cook at 325 degrees for about 17 minutes. Watch very closely as they burn easily! Makes 12 dozen.

Bulldog Bread
BILL & NAN O'LEARY

½ cup sugar
½ cup brown sugar
2 tsp. cinnamon
4 10 oz. cans refrigerated biscuits
¾ cup chopped pecans
6 tbsp. margarine, melted

Preheat oven to 325 degrees. Combine sugars and cinnamon in a plastic bag. Separate biscuits and cut into quarters. Place quartered biscuits in bag and shake to coat with sugar. Grease bundt pan and sprinkle bottom of pan with pecans. Place sugar-coated biscuits in pan and drizzle with margarine. Bake 30 to 35 minutes. Turn coffee cake carefully onto a round plate while hot.

> Who is the greatest Georgia football fan? Not sure, but if I had to pick one, I'd certainly consider Robert Westmoreland of Ellijay. You see his feelings out on his sleeve not loud but pointedly sincere. You hear his heart beating to "Glory, Glory to Ol' Georgia," and you know he is for real. I don't get to see him often, but whenever I go near Ellijay, I call him for a barbecue lunch.
>
> He has a drawl that makes me smile at the sound

of his voice. He used to take me and Georgia offensive coordinator, the late Bill Pace, on overnight fishing excursions in the Chattoochee National Forest. The premature death of his son, Rob, almost did him in. But he rallied and today, sells insurance for Cotton States, works for the good of his community and follows the Dogs.

I just like Robert Westmoreland. I like his style, I like his enthusiasm and I like to be around him.

Mushroom Logs
MYRA THOMAS

2 cans Pillsbury refrigerated crescent rolls
8 oz. Cream cheese
4 to 5 oz. jar sliced mushrooms
1 tsp. seasoned salt
1 egg (beaten)
Poppy seeds

The crescent rolls should be pressed together to form 8 rectangles. Mix the cream cheese, mushrooms and seasoned salt together and spread on the 8 rectangles. Roll the crescent rolls jelly-roll style long ways. Slick each roll into about 6 or 7 bite size pices. Brush each piece with the egg and sprinkle with the poppy seeds. Bake at 425 degrees until golden brown. Best when served warm.

Cheese and Pimento Biscuits
JANIE & CODY GUNN

3 cups flour, sifted
5 teaspoons baking powder
1½ teaspoons salt
½ teaspoon cayenne pepper
½ cup shortening
1 cup cheddar cheese, grated (add more to taste)
¼ cup pimento, finely chopped
1 to 1½ cups milk

Preheat oven to 450 degrees. Sift together dry ingredients in large bowl. Cut in shortening. Stir in cheese and add milk gradually to make dough. Roll out to ½-inch thickness. Cut with biscuit cutter and place on greased cookie sheet. Bake 15 minutes. Can be prepared ahead and frozen after baking. Reheat before serving. Makes 3 dozen.

Almond biscotti
GAIL & DON PERNO

⅓ cup butter (salted or unsalted)
⅔ cup sugar
2 cups flour
2 eggs
2 tsp. baking powder
2 tsp. vanilla
1½ cups slivered almonds

Grind ¾ cup slivered almonds very fine in mini chopper

continued

or food processor and mix with flour. Grind the other ³/₄ cup not as fine (small pieces). In mixing bowl beat butter with electric mixer on medium speed 30 seconds or until softened. Add 1 cup flour, sugar, baking powder, vanilla and one egg at a time. Stir in remaining flour and nuts. Mix just until the dough clings together. Do not over-work it. Divide dough in half and shape into 2 logs with lightly floured hands. Logs should be 9 inches long and 2 inches wide. Place logs on sprayed baking sheet. Bake in preheated 350 degrees oven for 25 minutes. Cool on cookie sheet. When cool cut with a serrated knife. Slice diagonally at a 45 degree angle about ¹/₂-inch thick. Lay the cookies flat on a greased cookie sheet and bake 325 degrees for 18 to 20 minutes. Let cool on rack.

Chocolate Glaze variation

1 cup milk
Chocolate or semisweet chocolate pieces
2 tbsp. shortening

Melt chocolate and shortening in double boiler or microwave. Stir to blend. Dip the tops of cookies in chocolate and let stand on wax paper to set.

VEGGIES & CASSEROLES

U of Ga. 1892 Football Team

| A. O. HALSEY. | E. P. HOWELL, Jr. | E. W. FREY. | GEO. SHACKLEFORD. | R. B. NALLEY. |
| JULIAN R. LANE. | F. J. HERTY. | W. N. GRAMLING. | H. C. BROWN. | J. C. KIMBALL. | L. D. FRICKS |

In the beginning . . .

Country Fried Corn

MICHELE CLOVIS

Bacon (fried and chopped) (save the grease)
2 cans sweet Gawga corn kernel (drained)
1 tsp. sugar
Salt and pepper
1 tsp. butter

Make this in an iron skillet. Fry bacon until crisp and remove from skillet. Add corn and sugar and butter to drippings in skillet. Salt and pepper. Crumble bacon back into the skillet. Cover and simmer for 30 minutes on medium heat. You can also add whole frozen green beans to this if you like. Unbelievable dish! I like it just flash fried so the corn is crisp.

Gary Couvillion is Georgia's faculty chairman of athletics, a smiling, grinning character whose accent makes you realize right off that you are in the presence of a real Cajun. For years he and his wife, Nancy, maintained serious emotional devotion to the LSU Tigers. After living in Athens all these years, however they have become avid fans of the 'Dogs. LSU is no longer a factor with their college football emotions.

If you know anything about LSU football history, you know what it must have been like in Baton Rouge on Halloween night in 1959 when the legendary Billy Cannon took a punt 89-yards to win a classic SEC battle over Ole Miss.

Gary and Nancy, not married at the time, were

on a hayride that night. They celebrated into the evening as you would expect two avid Tiger fans to do.

Years later when Nancy met Cannon, she told him where they were that night, and then quipped: "You scored that night but he (Gary) didn't."

Cajun Grits

NANCY & GARY COUVILLON

1 cup grits
3 cups boiling water
1 6oz. Roll garlic cheese (Kraft)
1 stick butter or margarine
3 eggs well beaten
⅔ cup milk
⅓ cup grated cheddar cheese

Cook grits in water. When done add cheese and butter. Stir until melted. Let cool slightly. Mix together eggs and milk. Add to grits mixture. Put grated cheese on top. Bake in baking dish. Cover with aluminum foil. Spray underside of foil with vegetable spray to prevent cheese from sticking to foil. Bake at 350 degrees for 40 minutes. Last 15 minutes uncover. Serves 8

I also add Tabasco to the milk mixture because we like it spicy.

I double this recipe and put in a 9" x 11" Pyrex dish. To triple, use a 11" x 13" dish. This may be made ahead and kept in refrigerator but will take longer to cook.

I've never tried to learn whether Vince Dooley can cook anything or not. But what I do know is that he can eat. Man can he eat! If you push back your plate with food on it, Vince will fork what you leave.

Through the years Myrna and I have enjoyed a lot of good times with Vince and Barbara. We vacationed with them, Bill and Ruth Hartman, in Jamaica for many years.

That was Vince at his finest. Swimming in the Caribbean, jogging on the beach, taking long naps after lunch and enjoying pre-dinner cocktails in the Hartman suite at the Casa Blanca Hotel at Montego Bay.

Vince, Bill and I often flew to Port Antonio and rafted down the Rio Grande River with our rafts loaded down with Red Stripe beer plus a good supply of scotch.

If you were drinking scotch, you could pour yourself a drink and then dip over the side into the river for your water. Although Red Stripe was my choice, I do say there has never been a better scotch and water than on the Rio Grande.

At the time when we started going to Jamaica, Hartman, who had the worst swing in golf, had not given up the game. We talked Vince into to playing with us one day at the Tryal Club. A mongoose ran across the fairway and Vince tried to get his caddie to tell him the plural of mongoose. Is it mongooses or mongeese? "Okay," Vince said. "When we saw that one run across the fairway, I said, there goes one mongoose. If two run across the fairway, what do you say? The caddie replied, "There go two mongoose, mon."

Carrot Soufflé

BARBARA & VINCE DOOLEY

3 tbsp. butter
3 tbsp. flour
1 cup hot milk
¼ tsp. salt
3 eggs
2 cups cooked carrots, mashed (about 2 lbs. carrots)
1 tsp. vanilla
3 tbsp. sugar
½ tsp. nutmeg

In mixing bowl blend melted butter and flour. Add milk and mix until smooth. Add remaining ingredients. Pour mixture into a greased casserole. Bake at 350 degrees for 40 minutes. Serves 6.

Southern Style Tomato Pudding

JERRY & LEE EPTING

3 16 oz. Cans diced tomatoes
1½ cups shredded cheddar cheese
⅓ cup sliced green onion
2 tbsp. Sugar
6 slices white bread torn into pieces
Salt and pepper to taste

Toss all ingredients together; pour into a lightly greased pyrex baking dish. Bake at 300 degrees for 20 to 25 minutes. Serves 12 to 16.

Nobody thought Billy Payne could pull off the Olympics but he, with Bulldog tenacity, got it done. He wore No. 87 playing on both sides of the ball at some point during his Bulldog career. He made All-SEC in 1968 as a defensive end.

Jack Stephens, Chairman of the Augusta National Golf Club, was so impressed with Billy when they met to talk about golf becoming part of the Olympics that he invited Billy to join the Augusta National Golf Club. When Hootie Johnson became Chairman he assigned Billy as head of the press and public relations committee, succeeding Charlie Yates, former winner of the British Amateur championship.

Everybody who knew Billy at Georgia, knew that he was going to move in high circles. Today, an Atlanta businessman, Billy remains vitally interested in his alma mater. He serves on numerous committees and at age 54 he is an accomplished and devoted alumnus with plenty of time left to work for his alma mater.

Vidalia Onion Delight

BILLY & MARTHA PAYNE

4 to 5 large Vidalia onions, sliced in thin rings (Walla Walla sweets if you must)
2 cups sugar
4 cups water
1 cup white vinegar

Dissolve sugar in water and add vinegar. Put onion rings in mixture and marinate at least four hours.

Drain. Coat with ½ to ¾ cup of mayonnaise. Add 2 to 3 teaspoons of celery salt and toss.

Serve on crackers as hors d'oeuvres or on salads or sandwiches.

Tomato Stuff

BOB & JEANE ARGO

3 pcs. Bacon
1 large onion (chopped)
1 large can diced tomatoes (drain off half of liquid)
3 slices white bread
¼ cup butter
2 to 3 tablespoons sugar
Salt and pepper to taste

Fry bacon crisp and remove from skillet. Brown onions in bacon drippings. Add onion and drippings to tomatoes in casserole dish. Brown crumbled bread in ¼ cup butter (melted). Add to tomato mixture. Season with sugar, salt and pepper. Bake in 350 degrees oven uncovered for 40 to 45 minutes. I double recipe because it's good left over.

Sister's Marinated Green Beans

KEITH & LINDA JERKINS

3 cans whole Blue Lake green beans (drained)
2 purple onions (slicked thinly)

Cook beans for five minutes in salted water. Drain

continued

beans. Layer beans and onions in casserole dish.

Marinade

2 ²/₃ cups sugar
2 ²/₃ cups white vinegar
1 ¹/₃ cups water
5 tbs. vegetable oil
salt and pepper to taste

Combine ingredients and boil for five minutes. Pour over beans and onions, and chill for twenty-four hours. Drain and serve cold or at room temperature. Serves 8 to 10.

Susan B's Buttered Beans

JOHNNY & MARY ANNA TERRELL

2 cans pork and beans
1 can lima beans
1 can kidney beans
1 can great northern beans
2 large chopped onions, preferably Vidalia
¹/₂ cup brown sugar
2 teaspoons brown mustard
¹/₃ cup cider vinegar

Put beans in large casserole dish. Sauté onions with butter. Add sugar, mustard and vinegar to onions. Stir, then pour over beans. Put bacon on top and bake at 350 degrees for 1 hour.

Roadside Potatoes

KATHY DAY WESTMORELAND

6 cubed raw potatoes
¹/₂ cup onion (chopped fine)
¹/₂ green pepper (chopped fine)
2 cups grated sharp cheddar cheese
2 to 3 cups milk
Margarine, flour, salt and pepper

Mix potatoes with onions and green pepper. Add salt and pepper to taste. In a 2 quart baking dish, layer the potato mixture with 1 tbsp. flour, a few pats of margarine and some cheddar cheese. Continue layering (probably 3 times). Add milk to barely cover potato mixtures. Bake uncovered at 350 degrees for about one hour or until potatoes are done. I make this the night before the game and cook it. Then I warm it up in microwave before we leave and wrap it in foil. They taste great even when barely warm! This can easily be doubled.

Red Beans and Rice

GARY & NANCY COUVILLON

Boil small ham with bone until falls off bone. Save broth.
Render four slices of bacon. Remove bacon. Into bacon drippings add 3 tablespoons butter. Chop and add 2 cups purple onion, 1¹/₂ cup celery, 1 cup bell pepper, 7 cloves or garlic. Sauté until wilted. Add 1 lb. small red beans and sauté a little bit. Add enough broth and/or water to beans. Add salt, Cajun seasoning, Tabasco, black and red pepper or broth to taste. Add two bay leaves. Cook beans covered about 45 minutes. You

will probably have to add more broth/water as beans cook. Don't let liquid cook out. Add crumbled bacon, pieces of ham, and slices of smoked sausage (andouille if you can get it). Cook until done. Then mash some of the beans on the side of the pot to thicken gravy.

Serve over cooked white long grain rice. Sprinkle chopped green onions on top if desired.

Potluck Beans

JoAn & TONY SALLOUM

1 lb. ground beef
1 cup chopped onion

Brown and drain the ground beef and onion. Put mixture in 4 quart crock pot along with:

¾ lb. Little Smokie sausages
2 cans pork and beans
1 can kidney beans, drained
1 can lima beans
1 cup ketchup
3 tbsp. white vinegar

Cook at 200 degrees (low) for 4 to 5 hours. Stir once while cooking.

Potluck Potatoes

GAIL ROBERTSON

Boil 10 to 15 potatoes with peeling on. Cool enough to cut up in chunks. Spray large casserole with Pam or just coat with margarine. Layer the following ingredients.

2 cut up onions
1 bell pepper
¾ lb. cubed cheese
2 to 3 cloves garlic, chopped
Jar (small or large, suit your taste) drained pimentos
Salt and pepper to taste
Spicy paprika (or whatever spice you like — it's pot luck, remember!)
About 4 little chunks of margarine
A little garlic salt

Bake at 350 degrees about 40 minutes. Top with bread crumbs that you've mixed with melted margarine and garlic salt. Bake for another 10 minutes.

Hominy Casserole

TINA & TOMMY TINKER

1 medium onion, chopped
1 clove garlic, minced
1 tablespoon oil
1 cup sour cream
¾ cup shredded cheddar cheese, divided
¼ cup milk
1 (4 oz.) can chopped green chilies
¼ teaspoon ground cumin
3 (15 oz.) cans golden hominy, drained

In a small skillet, cook onion and garlic in oil until tender. Remove from heat. In a bowl, combine onion mixture,

continued

sour cream, half of the cheese, milk, chilies and cumin. Add hominy; mix well. Pour into a greased 2-qt. baking dish. Bake, uncovered, at 350 degrees for 30 minutes or until heated through. Sprinkle with remaining cheese. Serve immediately.

> *Jill Arrington, the blond bombshell who reports from the sideline for CBS college football games, grew up in Conyers and has always been a devoted Georgia fan even though she enrolled at Miami. Her affinity for the Bulldogs comes natural. Her father, Rick, lettered at Georgia in 1966. Recently married, Jill has enjoyed her trips to Athens through the years. She travels constantly in her work. But she doesn't get shut out in the kitchen.*

Easy Cheese Potato Casserole

JILL ARRINGTON

1 bag frozen hashbrown potatoes (2 lbs. chopped)
1 can cream of chicken soup
2 cups sour cream
2 cups sharp cheddar cheese, grated
1 stick butter, melted
1 tablespoon salt

Preheat oven to 375 degrees. Grease 9" x 13" pan. Mix all ingredients in a bowl except butter. Pour mixture into pan. Pour melted butter over top of casserole. Bake for 1 hour.

Breakfast Casserole

NAN & BILL O'LEARY

12 slices white bread
1 lb. Bulk sausage (mild)
1 jar Kraft Old English cheese spread
Chunks of Velveta cheese
3 cups milk
1 tsp. dry mustard
½ tsp. seasoned salt
Cornflakes

Place 6 slices of bread (no crust) on bottom of greased casserole dish. Brown and drain sausage and place on bread. Put cheese chunks all over. Place remaining six slices of bread (no crust) on top. Mix milk, eggs, mustard and seasoned salt together and pour over top. Cover with crushed Cornflakes. Cover and refrigerate overnight. Cook at 450 degrees for 45 minutes uncovered.

> *John Henry Terrell Jr., with advanced age creeping on, is no longer a kid. But you wouldn't know it when football season comes around. In fact, his nickname is "Kid." That is how everybody knows him.*
>
> *At the Cotton Bowl in 1976 soul singer James Brown, who like the Kid is from Toccoa, showed up at practice one day. "Has anybody seen Kid Terrell, Brown asked?" Then looking around, added. "I thought he would be at practice today."*
>
> *All of Kid's friends find him to be the most delightful and lovable character they know. Count me in that group.*

Kid runs the best-known Tailgate Club at Sanford Stadium. You can't participate unless you are a dues paying member or the guest of somebody who is. If you are a member and try to slip by without anteing up, Kid knows. If you come without your cooler and try to sneak a beer or a Jack Daniels from someone else, Kid's eagle eye will stare you down.

He glories in the start of football season. He sends out notices with a streamer across the top of the page, "I Hate Tech." His friends know that is literally true.

Kid does love the Bulldogs. He doesn't want to be on the athletic board, he doesn't want to be invited to Mark Richt's house. He doesn't want any publicity. He just wants the Bulldogs to win so he can party and celebrate with his friends.

With his great affection for the Dogs, how in the world did he miss the winning touchdown in Knoxville last year? When Tennessee scored late, he and a couple of friends headed to their car, to get ahead of the traffic. They made a vow not to let anybody know what they had done. But somebody figured it out and made an issue out of it. "I'll never live it down," Kid said.

Perhaps, Kid is the most successful country banker there is. He makes money and he's got money. But he doesn't live extravagantly. He counts his accumulation devotedly, but he spends wisely and conservatively. His friends kid the Kid often about his frugality. But let's go on record that you could label Kid as "tight." But he is not cheap like a couple of his friends who shall remain nameless.

A story everybody loves has to do with the Butts-Mehre campaign. I was on the point asking for money to build the building. Kid often sent me his balance sheet, a summary that showed how successful the Merchants and Farmers Bank of Comer

had been in the last year. I made my pitch. "Kid why don't you help us do a tribute to Coach (Bill) Hartman. You love Bill and you all have had a lot of fun with him over the years. With all that money you are making you could donate $25,000 easily. You could install it over a five-year period. You wouldn't miss it."

He grinned and said, "Yep I could give it, but I'd sure miss it."

Kid's Baked Beans

JOHN & ELINOR TERRELL

2 large cans spicey pork and beans
½ onion, chopped
½ cup brown sugar
½ cup cane or other heavy syrup
2 tbsp. yellow mustard
½ cup catsup
dash chili seasoning
Bacon for topping

Mix all ingredients in a large casserole or iron skillet. Cook at 350 degrees for one hour or more until most of the liquid is absorbed. Serves 20 plus.

Served at Kid's hamburger tailgate cook-out and with E.H.'s fine ribs!

One thing you have to say about Georgia President Michael Adams. He does like sports. Additionally, he likes to win. It bugs him when the Bulldogs lose, and he sticks out his chest with the best of us when victories and championships come about. He is also a fan of his wife's culinary skills. Mary is a good cook and here are a couple of her tailgate favorites.

Mixed Bean Casserole

MARY & MICHAEL ADAMS

8 slices bacon (fried crisp) (or can use can of Read
    Bacon Bits as shortcut)
1 onion, chopped and cooked until limp
1 can (1lb.) Cut green beans
1 can (1 lb.) Pork and beans
1 can (1 lb.) Red kidney beans
1 can (1 lb.) butter beans (green or yellow)

Drain all beans except pork and beans and combine.
    Then Add:

1 cup ketchup (less if pork and beans are real juicy)
1 cup brown sugar
3 tbsp. vinegar
¼ tsp. salt
1 tsp. dry mustard
1 tbsp. Worcestershire sauce

Add onions and bacon. Mix gently. Place in slightly greased casserole dish. Bake at 325 degrees for 1 hour.

Easy Chicken Casserole

TINA & TOMMY TINKER

2 cups cooked chicken, cut into pieces
1 can condensed cream of chicken soup
1 cup sour cream
32 Ritz crackers
¼ cup chopped onion
¼ cup chopped mushrooms

Put chicken in a greased 9" x 13" inch baking dish. Combine soup, sour cream, onion and mushrooms. Pour mixture over chicken and top with Ritz crackers. Cover and bake at 350 degrees for 30 minutes.

Shrimp Casserole

JOYCE BANKSTON

1 lb. shrimp, cooked
1 lb. cottage cheese
½ cup slivered almonds
½ cup parmesan cheese
½ cup crumbled saltines
½ lb. butter or oleo
Garlic salt

Sprinkle bottom of casserole generously with garlic salt. Place shrimp and cover with cottage cheese. Sprinkle in almonds and parmesan cheese. Cover with the crumbled saltines. Pour butter or oleo on top. Bake at 20 minutes at 350 degrees.

MEATS & SEAFOOD

I'm taking orders now!

All of us over the course of our college careers, usually experience more than one roommate.

One of my roommates was Fred Farah of Jacksonville. Freddy is Arabic. His father brought the family to North Florida from Ramallah, the West Bank capital which has been in the news so often. Freddy could not speak English which meant that, at school, he was the subject of many taunts. But his good nature and his generous style won everybody over. A jovial type, Freddy was a man with a big and generous heart. Freddy took up American football and played it very well. He was All-City and even though he was surrounded by all that Gator orange, he chose the Bulldogs.

At Payne Hall, where the athletes on scholarship lived, everybody enjoyed Freddy. We called him "Camel Driver" because of his Middle East heritage. Freddy didn't mind being the butt of jokes, he even poked fun at himself, topping off any comment with a hearty laugh. Only problem with rooming with Freddy was that when he slept on his back, his snoring would shake the walls.

Theron Sapp roomed directly above us and when Freddy's snoring peaked, Sapp often would take a metal object and beat on the exposed pipes that ran down the walls of our rooms. "Turn over Camel Driver," Sapp would scream. When Freddy slept on his stomach he did not snore.

Freddy had pretty much learned English in the street which meant that while he was able to communicate, and well, things like writing themes could be overwhelming. I worked with him on his themes, and with gritty determination, he passed. Had he not gotten through English he would have been denied a degree. Freddy was determined to obtain a degree.

From the day he left Georgia, he has remained one of the Bulldogs most devoted fans. He has contributed generously to numerous Bulldog causes and has always bought season tickets. He was among the first six figure donors to the Butts-Mehre campaign.

When I knew I would be making a trip to the Middle East, I called Freddy and he called his cousin in the West Bank. His cousin came to my hotel in Jerusalem and took me into the West Bank. I invited Vince Dooley to go with me and we had a very pleasant time. Learned a lot from that trip and what I remember about crossing the border into Ramallah was the stunning display of fruits and vegetables at the street market.

Anybody who hails from Ramallah knows how to cook. By rooming with Freddy Farah, I was the beneficiary of wonderful pastries his family would ship to him at Payne Hall. When he opened the box, the athletes would gather around and dig in. No problem with Freddy. He was willing to share with his Bulldog friends.

Nothing has changed in that regard over the years.

Lamb on Skewers

FREDDY & BRENDA FARAH

3 lbs. boned lean leg of lamb or round staek
3 large onions, quartered
1 cup wine
2 tablespoons oil
1 tablespoon dried mint
Salt and pepper to taste
4 green peppers, sliced
5 to 6 medium tomatoes

continued

Cut lamb or steak into 1½ inch squares. Make a marinade of onions, wine, oil, and mint in a deep dish and marinate meat for at least 2 hours, preferably overnight. Season when ready to broil. Arrange lamb squares on skewers, alternating with onion, pepper slices, and tomato slices. Broil slowly over hot charcoals or in a broiler on kitchen range, about 10 minutes. Serves 8 to 10.

Bat Varnadoe hails from Savannah, a genuine character who often comes to games dressed as Bat Man. He once told me. "You are the envy of all your friends. All of us love Georgia like you, but you stayed in Athens and worked for the Dogs. Every last one of us would like to do what you do." I confess to being guilty.

For years before returning to Savannah, he lived in Oakland, Ca. I once spent the night at his house on a West Coast trip. Did we have fun, sipping beer and talking about our Georgia days?

Bat comes to Athens as often as he can. He is the quintessential sophomore. He talked his KA fraternity brothers into letting him build a loft in the stairwell of the house on North Lumpkin. And when he is in town, that is where he sleeps.

Walking Chili Dogs a la Varsity
GORDON VARNEDOE

1. Enough money to purchase chilidogs in quantity adequate to serve the number of expected guest and extra for unexpected guest.
2. A volunteer with transportation to go to the Varsity and order the chili dogs "walking," (i.e. to take out).

Serve as Hors d'eouvres or as main course depending on tailgate budget.

Editor's note:
A lifelong student who by his own admission has never mentally gotten out of college, Gordon "Bat" Varnedoe was a Bulldog walk-on in 1960. He has been known to show up at Homecoming in his batman costume to sing with Clisby Clarke on the Tailgate Show. His grandfather Gordon Saussy was head coach in 1899 at 26.

Skewered Fitzyshrimp
JENNIFER & MIKE FITZGERALD

2 lbs. St. Simons Island local shrimp peeled and deveined

Marinate overnight
Juice of 4 limes
Handful of basil, finely chopped
1 clove garlic, diced
Coating of extra virgin olive oil

Grill preparation—very important.

Exactly 35 Kingsford coals single layered in a Weber grill, should take up about ⅓ of bottom rack. Wait until coals go beyond the hottest part of the burn, on their way down.

Then, skewer the shrimp with water-soaked medium sized sticks. Grill shrimp as slow as possible, should take 20 minutes if done right, may have to move shrimp off direct heat and close lid with vents closed about ⅔.

In the final two minutes of cooking, toss some sea salt and cracked pepper on the shrimp, a very light dusting of cayenne pepper is nice if the Coronas taste exceptionally well that day.

This recipe can be served cold or hot, but my favorite is just served.

Shrimp 'Etouffee
KATHY & BRENT CRYMES

2 lbs unpeeled medium-size fresh shrimp
3 cups water
2 cups chopped onions
4 cloves garlic, minced
2 tablespoons butter or margarine, melted
1 cup sliced green onions
3 tablespoons cornstarch
⅓ cup chopped fresh parsley
¾ teaspoon salt
¼ teaspoon ground white pepper
Hot cooked rice

Peel and devein shrimp, reserving shells and tails. Chop shrimp, and set aside. Place shells and tails in a medium saucepan; add water, and bring to a boil. Cover, reduce heat, and simmer 30 minutes. Pour liquid through a wire mesh strainer into a bowl, discarding shells and tails. Set strained stock aside.

Cook chopped onion and garlic in butter in a large skillet over medium-high heat, stirring constantly, until tender. Add 2 cups of the reserved stock, and bring to a boil. Reduce heat to low; stir in shrimp and green onions. Cook 5 minutes, stirring occasionally.

Combine cornstarch and an additional ½ cup reserved stock; gradually stir into shrimp mixture. Bring to a boil; boil, stirring constantly 1 minute. Stir in parsley, salt, and pepper. Serve over rice. Makes 8 servings.

True friendships endure, Myrna and I have never had a more wonderful friend than Vernon Brinson, a little man with a big heart. Now a very successful automobile dealer in New Orleans, he makes frequent trips back to Athens in the fall to see the Bulldogs play.

He is past President and Chairman of the Sugar Bowl, and when Herschel Walker led the team to New Orleans three years in a row, winning the National Championship in 1980, nobody was prouder than Vernon. He introduced Peyton Manning to Herschel when Peyton was in grade school. Peyton always said that Georgia was his second favorite team (after Ole Miss).

My favorite story about Vernon, who lettered in baseball for Coach Jim Whatley, has to do with Whatley making him the final member of the squad in 1958. In those days the total number of players on the team corresponded to the number of uniforms available. When Whatley got down to the last uniform he gave it to Vernon, who stood all of 5-8. The uniform he gave Vernon would have fit the 6-6 Whatley himself.

Vernon, nonetheless, was the proudest member of the team. He took his uniform to Dick Ferguson's to have it taken up. The tailor tried hard but when it was over with, the pants were as baggy as you could imagine. The pants gathered around his ankles.

One day Whatley sent his bighearted catcher up to pinch hit. The pitcher threw three straight pitches that literally bounced across the plate but the ump called them all strikes. This caused the colorful Whatley to bound out of the dugout and ask the ump what was going on. "All three of those balls bounced across the plate," Whatley said. The grinning ump replied, "But coach they still were above his knees."

Recently Vernon endowed a scholarship in Coach Whatley's memory, another expression of his deep and abiding love for the University of Georgia.

Vernon and his wife, Patricia, know about good food, coming from New Orleans. Their favorite spot, like with so many New Orleans natives, is Galatoire's. Unless they are in Athens. Even late at night following a big game Vernon heads to the Varsity where he orders a few chili dogs.

Shrimp Appetizer
VERNON & PATRICIA BRINSON

6 lbs. Raw shrimp in shells
2 bay leaves
1 tsp. Celery seed
¾ cup salt
1 tsp. Cayenne pepper
2 cups oil
½ cup catsup
3 tbs. lemon juice
¼ cup apple cider vinegar
1 tbs. Worcestershire sauce
1 5-oz. Jar fresh horseradish
1 5-oz. Jar hot Creole mustard
1 cup thinly sliced yellow onion
Salt and pepper to taste

Make this a day ahead. In a large pot, place shrimp, cover with water. Add bay leaves, celery seed, cayenne and salt. Bring to a boil and cook five minutes until shrimp are pink. Drain and peel. Combine remaining ingredients. Add shrimp. Cover and refrigerate. Serve with toothpicks or on crackers.

Shrimp Cakes and Watercress Remoulade
KIM & LEE BARTON

Shrimp cakes ingredients:
⅓ cup butter
½ small sweet onion, minced
½ cup all purpose flour
2 cups milk
1 tablespoon seafood seasonings
½ teaspoon ground red pepper
2 large eggs, lightly beaten
4 cups chopped cooked shrimp
1 cup saltine crackers, crushed
½ cup vegetable oil

Watercress remoulade

1½ cups mayonnaise
2 tablespoon Dijon mustard
1 bunch watercress, chopped
3 green onions, sliced
½ cup chopped fresh chives
1 garlic clove, minced
¼ teaspoon ground red pepper
Stir together and chill.

Melt butter in large saucepan over medium heat; add onion and sauté 3 minutes or until onion is tender. Whisk in flour, whisking constantly about 1 minute. Gradually add milk and whisk constantly until thickened. Remove from heat and stir in seafood seasoning and red pepper.

Cool mixture. After cooled, whisk in beaten eggs; stir in shrimp and cracker crumbs.

Shape into 16 or 32 patties. Chill 2 hours. Cook in 2 batches in hot oil in large skillet over medium heat. Cook 4-5 minutes on each side or until golden brown. Drain on paper towels. Serve with chilled watercress mayonnaise.

Sally's Fried Chicken
MARTHA TRAMMELL WYANT

1 chicken, cup up, or a pack of your favorite pieces, remove skin for less fat
4 cups flour in paper bag
Crisco oil
2 eggs and 2 tblpns. milk, whisk together for egg wash
Lawry's season salt
Salt and pepper to taste
Garlic powder

Pour enough oil in deep fryer to fill ½ full. Turn on high.

Lay chicken out on rack over sink and season on both sides with Lawry's, salt, pepper and garlic. Put groups of 3 to 4 pieces in egg wash and then in bag of flour. Shake, shake, shake. Leave in bag about 1 minute. Put in fryer. Fry in batches about 15 to 20 minutes until golden brown. Dry on paper towels. Serve hot, cold or room temperature.

Pickled Shrimp
KIRBY MOORE

1 tablespoon dry mustard
¼ cup salt
1 teaspoon red pepper
¼ box celery seed
¼ bottle Tabasco sauce
1 quart vinegar
2½ lbs. medium unpeeled shrimp

Prior to boiling shrimp in above ingredients, soak shrimp in a separate mixture of salty water for 30 minutes then drain and follow directions.

Place all ingredients (except shrimp) in a large pot of water and bring to a boil. Add shrimp and boil for 15 minutes. Drain. Enjoy with garlic bread and a mixture of melted butter and garlic salt for dipping. Be sure to have a cold beverage on had, this concoction has been known to make you thirsty.

Sonny Seiler has such hard-edged passion for Georgia that I remember him screaming at his wife, Cecilia, after the Bulldogs lost a basketball game. He felt that she was not hurting like he was.

It gets to Sonny when Georgia loses any contest. He rants and raves at every negative headline. He knows for sure that there is an unfair bias against Georgia at the Atlanta Journal-Constitution sports department. He can feel it in his bones.

When I try to explain circumstances, he gets mad at me. "Don't defend the bastards," he will say. "You can't tell me they don't find ways to hurt Georgia and it fractures me to no end."

An accomplished practical joker, he was civil to me when his friend and neighbor, Remer Lane, and I, pulled off a remarkable practical joke on him during the late stages of Vince Dooley's coaching career. I wrote an apocryphal letter, supposedly from a Georgia fan who said he didn't like it that Uga didn't attend more basketball games and other team sports events.

With Sonny the Georgia mascot must be, and I repeat must be, an all white male English Bulldog.

In my fake letter to Coach Dooley the "Georgia fan" who had supposedly written it offered his bull-dog to fill in at basketball games, out-of-town foot-ball games Uga did not attend, and any other event that Uga couldn't make. I got Vince to scribble this in the margin: "Loran, please look into this. It sounds like something we ought to do." Then I mailed the letter to Sonny, marking it FYI. He hit the ceiling, and soon had my phone jumping off the hook. The fictitious author said his dog, Lilly, had a brindle spot surrounding her eye, everything the Seiler Ugas weren't. He was still steaming when after a game, I drove to Savannah to a party hosted by the Lanes. Sonny's friend, the late Johnny Peters, even had an

oil painting done of Lilly, with a bra.

Sonny, who has pulled so many jokes on so many of his friends, was done in by the Lilly episode. He took it good-naturedly and still has that oil painting of Lilly.

Looking after the Ugas has to be a labor of love. Such dogs are high maintenance, especially in Savannah's heat. The Dogs would be in trouble if it weren't for Cecilia who truly loves them. Sonny is out front taking bows but she is in the background looking after the Dogs.

Sometimes I think Uga realizes that.

Savannah Marinated Shrimp

CECILIA & SONNY SEILER

4 pounds peeled, cooked shrimp
1 cup Wesson oil
1 cup tarragon vinegar
2 cloves garlic crushed
2 medium onions sliced
Salt, black pepper and red pepper to taste.

Marinate in refrigerator overnight. Travels well in wide neck soup thermos. Serve with toothpicks and crackers.

Brisket

PAULA & SKIP CARAY

Skip is a member of the Braves broadcast team. His kids, Shayelyn and Chip, are both Georgia graduates. Chip is an announcer for the Chicago Cubs, succeeding his late and legendary grandfather, Harry Caray.

1 (3 lbs.) brisket
2 tablespoons garlic
1 tablespoon Hungarian paprika
1 package onion soup mix
1 (12 oz.) can regular Coke

Preheat oven to 350 degrees.

In a 9" x 13" pan, place brisket and sprinkle with garlic, paprika and soup mix. Pour Coke into pan, preferably not directly on the meat so as to not wash the seasonings off. Seal the pan very well with foil and bake for three hours.

After brisket has cooked, place entire pan in refrigerator overnight. Remove congealed fat from the pan. Slice thinly across the grain. Reheat the juices.

Serves about 6 people.

Larry Munson likes to eat. Mostly fish, quail, dove, duck, venison. He likes movies, the Bulldogs and a cold North wind unless he is fishing. People are always asking, "When will Larry retire?" He doesn't say. I vote for him to keep on going. The Georgia fans love him and his health is good. Why give up something you are good at?

He was born in Minneapolis, son of Harry Munson of Swedish decent. He was introduced to sports and outdoor life by his father. They hunted,

they fished, and they huddled by a radio, searching for the golden voice of Ted Husing, the great sportscasting pioneer.

A favorite story Munson uses today in his speeches concerns Husing's broadcast of a prizefight. Husing had placed a bet on one of the fighters, who got knocked cold in the first round. Startled, Husing blurted out, "Well, the dumb S.O.B. just got knocked out."

Instantly realizing what he had done, he turned his head aside and yelled into the microphone, "Hey, you can't talk like that! We're on the air!"

Munson's Wild Duck Recipe

LARRY MUNSON

A big pot of water has to be brought up to a boil on the stove…place one thawed out duck in the pot for exactly 60 seconds, no more no less. After 60 seconds the water in the pot will turn dirty and black. Remove the duck, rinse off thoroughly with cold water. Then place a slice of apple, orange, onion, potato and jam them up inside the cavity of the duck. Cook slowly, about 325 degrees, for almost two hours. Throw the fruit and vegetables away that were inside the duck. Do not use the water you cooked them in for gravy. The rich, dark meat should be falling off the breast and there is no dark meat anywhere in the world that can touch wild duck, PROVIDED you have par boiled that duck for 60 seconds first.

Munson's pleasant, quail and partridge recipe

LARRY MUNSON

Pour two cans or Campbell's chicken broth soup along with only one can of water into the bottom of your roaster. Place the birds down in the soup and cook them slowly at 350 degrees for at least two hours, maybe slightly more. Keep basting the birds. Do not use the soup for gravy after you finish. Pheasants and partridge will cook better if you use only the breasts, but keep the quail whole.

Marinated Shrimp

MARY VIRGINIA & HURLEY JONES

2 lbs. cooked and cleaned shrimp (Place shrimp in
   boiling salted water. Cook until just pink. Shell and
   clean shrimp.)
½ cup chopped fine green pepper
½ cup chopped onions
1 tablespoon chopped parsley
1 teaspoon dry mustard
1 clove garlic crushed with teaspoon of salt
1 cup thick French dressing
1 teaspoon Worcestershire sauce
Pinch of white pepper
1 tablespoon horseradish (optional)

Mix all together. Chill for about two hours. Serve cold.
   Makes 6 servings.

When we were in college, Truett Jarrard was in pre-med and I was in journalism. During the summer Truett and I searched for white-fringed beetles in our summer jobs with the Agricultural Research Service. Truett went on to become a doctor and his son, Trey, and our son, Kent, became close friends when they were members of the SAE fraternity at Georgia. Truett loved all of Trey's friends and he was always partying at the fraternity house, so much so that Trey's fraternity brothers nicknamed Truett "Dr. Party." Truett is retired today living at St. George Island, Fl. He gets back to his adopted hometown of Newnan for football season. He has a sky suite at Sanford Stadium and definitely fits in the category of "rabid" fan. Truett introduced me to Bruce Williams' tasty sausage. Although Bruce has passed away, his family still produces the sausage which, made it to the White House when Jimmy Carter was president. That came about because Attorney General, Griffin Bell, loved the sausage and had a good supply shipped up. The attorney general shared some with the White House press corps, telling them the sausage was an aphrodisiac. By the way, you can't get that sausage recipe. It's like the Coca Cola formula. Bruce's family won't let the recipe out. You can buy his sausage and it's worth it to make the trip to Haralson and pick up a batch.

Mother's Sticky Roasted Chicken

JULIETTE & TREY JARRARD

2 teaspoons salt
1 teaspoon paprika
¾ teaspoon cayenne pepper
½ teaspoon onion powder
½ teaspoon thyme
¼ teaspoon white pepper
¼ teaspoon garlic powder
¼ teaspoon black pepper
1 three pound chicken
chopped onion

Combine seasonings, sprinkle and rub all over chicken. Stuff chicken cavity with onion. Roast uncovered at 250 degrees about 5 hours, basting occasionally with juices until chicken is golden brown and tender.

Sashimi

RICHARD & JANE APPLEBY

Fresh aku (bonita) orako (tuna)

Slice fish into very thin slices. Arrange on a layer of shredded daikon (white radish). Top with parsley.

Sauce

Combine 1 tablespoon mustard, 1 tablespoon water and let stand for a few minutes to "hotten." Add ¼ cup shoyu and blend well.

Lomi Lomi

RICHARD & JANE APPLEBY

1 lb. aku, skinned and sliced, other fish may be used
1 large onion, sliced
1 stalk green onion, chopped
Salt to taste
2 medium tomatoes, cubed
1 tablespoon sesame seeds, toasted
1 tablespoon sesame oil
½ teaspoon ginger, minced

Place all ingredients in a large bowl. Let stand for 3 hours before serving.

Lomi Salmon

RICHARD & JANE APPLEBY

1 lb. salted salmon
5 tomatoes, pared and diced
10 green onions, sliced thin
1 medium onion, finely chopped
1 cup crushed ice

Soak salmon in water for 3 hours. Remove skin and bones. Shred. Combine salmon, tomatoes, green onion and onion. Lomi or knead, be sure it is well mixed. Chill thoroughly. Add ice before serving.

Laulau

RICHARD & JANE APPLEBY

⅓ lb. butter fish or salmon
1 lb. pork butt
16 luau leaves or 1 lb. spinach
Ti leaves

Cut fish into 4 pieces and soak in water for I hour. Cut pork butt into pieces. Prepare luau leaves (or spinach) by stripping off stem vein. Wash and remove any tough ribs from leaves. Place 2 leaves on a board, place 4 luau leaves in center and add 1 piece of fish and 1 piece of pork on top. Fold leaves over filling to make a bundle. Tie ends. Steam for 3 to 4 hours.

Walter White is a native of Toccoa and was a lineman for the Bulldog teams of the early fifties. He has been a season ticket purchaser since he graduated. You'd have to say Walter has been quite loyal since he has lived in such places as San Francisco, New Orleans, Dallas, Baton Rouge, Memphis and Orlando.

This made it difficult for him to get to Athens, but nothing like his assignments with Coca Cola in the last ten years: Istanbul, Warsaw, Vienna, Moscow and the Baltic states. Myrna and I visited the Whites in most of those international settings. The Whites were perfect hosts, and we didn't always drink Coca Cola, especially when the sun went down.

He retired last summer and he and his wife, Charlotte, settled in Athens.

Walter is a big man with a robust personality, but a couple of years ago, we were having breakfast

at my house, and I invited his friend and coach, Jim Whatley to join us. There was a lot of laughter and reminiscing. At one point Walter began to tell his old coach how much he appreciated his influence. But it was difficult as his eyes clouded up and his voice began to crack.

There is nothing more touching than a player who proudly displays emotion for his old coach.

Lamb Kebabs with Yogurt and Tomato Sauce

CHARLOTTE & WALTER WHITE

This is one of the most wonderful kebab dishes imaginable. The meat is marinated and grilled, then removed from the skewers and placed atop a bed of warmed pita bread that has been torn into large bite-sized pieces. Two sauces are then drizzled over the meat and bread, a spicy tomato sauce and a yogurt-and-garlic sauce. As if this isn't enough, a little melted butter seasoned with cayenne pepper and paprika and a few strips of hot green chilies crown the dish. The long green peppers Turkish cooks use are not easily found outside of Turkey, so poblano chilies have been substituted here.

2 lbs. lamb sirloin, trimmed and cut into 1-inch cubes
½ cup plus 2 tablespoons olive oil
¼ cup grated onion
2 cloves garlic, minced, plus 2 tsp. finely minced garlic
2 tablespoons fresh lemon juice
1 tablespoon chopped fresh thyme
4 or 5 tomatoes

Pinch of red pepper flakes, crushed
Dash of red wine vinegar
Salt
6 tablespoon unsalted butter
1½ cups plain yogurt
Freshly ground pepper
4 large pita breads
Paprika
Cayenne pepper for seasoning butter
2 fresh poblano chilies, roasted, peeled, seeded and
*   diced or cut into long strips*

Place the lamb in a non-reactive container. In a small bowl stir together the ½ cup oil, onion, the 2 cloves minced garlic, lemon juice and thyme. Pour over the lamb, turn to coat well, cover and marinate in the refrigerator for several hours, or preferably overnight.

Heat cast-iron skillet over medium heat. Add the tomatoes and roast, turning, until blistered on all sides, about 4 minutes. Remove from the heat and, when cool enough to handle, peel, chop and put into a saucepan. Add the 2 tablespoons oil and the pepper flakes and cook over medium heat for about 5 minutes. Add the vinegar and salt to taste. Set aside and keep warm.

In a small sauté pan over medium heat, melt 2 tablespoons of the butter. Add the finely minced garlic and sauté for 1 to 2 minutes. Remove from the heat and let cool, then combine it with the yogurt in a small bowl. Add salt to taste and stir well. Cover and refrigerate, but bring to room temperature before serving.

Bring the lamb to room temperature. Prepare a fire in a charcoal grill.

Remove the lamb cubes from the marinade and thread onto skewers. Sprinkle with salt and pepper. Place on grill turning once, until done to taste, about 4 minutes on each side for medium-rare.

Meanwhile, warm the pita bread by wrapping it in aluminum foil and placing it on the grill rack for 7 minutes. Tear it into pieces and arrange on 4 individual plates. Melt the remaining 4 tablespoons butter and add paprika and cayenne to taste.

Reheat the tomato sauce. Top the bread with some of the warm tomato sauce and the yogurt sauce. Divide the lamb evenly among the plates. Top with the remaining tomato and yogurt sauces. Drizzle with the seasoned melted butter and the chilies. Serve at once.

JG's BBQ Ribs

JON GOLDSTEIN

3 racks of baby back ribs
2 bottles of BBQ sauce of choice
White vinegar
Tabasco sauce
Crushed red pepper
Black pepper
Garlic powder
Sugar
Honey
Napkins

Mix BBQ sauce, half cup vinegar, lots of Tabasco, lots of red pepper, lots of black pepper, lots of garlic powder, some sugar and some honey. Mix. Taste. Add to your liking. The hotter the better, it loses a little kick on the grill.

Bring ribs to a boil and boil for 25 minutes. Let cool (30 minutes). DRENCH ribs in sauce and allow to marinate as long as possible (preferably over night).

Grill ribs 10 to 15 minutes per side until perfect.

Gator Giggin Hot Dawgs

JERRY & GRACE AUSTIN

2 packages Bryans Smoked Lil Links (baby sausages)
2 (24 oz.) bottles Kraft Catalina dressing
4 tablespoons brown sugar
½ teaspoon garlic salt
¼ cup Worcestershire sauce
1½ tablespoon Lea & Perrins Sweet 'N Spicy Steak Sauce
1 large Vidalia onion, chopped

In medium skillet add 1 tablespoon butter. When butter begins to melt add onions, garlic salt and Bryans lil links slow cooking only to brown links and sauté onions about 10 to 15 minutes. Add Catalina dressing, and other ingredients together in a large crock pot and turn on high. Add ingredients from the skillet and when mixture begins to simmer turn to low and enjoy. We usually start this early Saturday morning before the game. It's a tailgate staple that has been enjoyed by all for many years.

Add the toothpicks and gig them gators!

Fried Salmon out of a can!

GAIL ROBERTSON

Drain salmon and remove bones (unless you're like me— I like them and leave them in!)

Flake a chunk of salmon off, big enough to fry.

Carefully sprinkle flour over the salmon that has been seasoned with salt/pepper/spices if you like. Have grease hot (300 degrees at least). Fry until crisp.

When Mark Richt came to Georgia, nobody had to tell him that he needed to win a championship.

That was obvious. The last time the Bulldogs had won an SEC title was in 1982. Georgia had never played in the Southeastern Conference championship game. Bulldog fans were hungry indeed. When we won the SEC East this season and defeated Arkansas for the title and the right to play in the Sugar Bowl, every wearer of the Red and Black was euphoric. It's not just that the championship drought had ended, loyal followers see a consistency of success on the horizon.

Mark Richt, not only is a winner, he has put fun back into the program.

He has brought a toughness to the program. Georgia had become a soft football team. Under Richt they have toughened up. They play a hard-nosed brand of ball and that is the direction Georgia needed to go.

I have been telling Bulldog clubs around the state that he has three basic interests: family, church and coaching. He works hard at each one of them.

He loves sitting with a tape machine reviewing Georgia tapes and tapes of opponents. Whatever you say about him, you have to say that Mark Richt is a football coach in the purest terms.

Hot Dawg Delite

COACH MARK & KATHARYN RICHT

Bread of your choice
Hot Dogs
Sliced Cheese
Baked Beans

Toast the bread on both sides in oven. Slice hot dogs on bread, cover with sliced cheese. Melt the cheese under the broiler and then add as many baked beans as possible. Throw a little ketchup on top. Serves as many as you want. You must use a fork…too sloppy to eat with hands! Tip: Use plenty of napkins.

Theron Sapp is one football player who truly wanted to play the game. After breaking his neck in high school in a swimming accident, Coach Wallace Butts told him he still had his scholarship. He recovered and started a four-win streak over Georgia Tech by scoring the touchdown that broke the drought on Grant Field in 1957. He was a tough runner and played 6 years in the NFL. After his NFL career ended, he settled in Augusta where he owned several fast food restaurants. He retired recently from the food business but will always be remembered for his touchdown that broke the drought.

His jersey, No. 40, was retired because the Georgia people loved him so much and were so grateful for his breaking the drought.

Grilled Beef Tenderloin

KAY & THERON SAPP

Marinate tenderloin for 30 minutes in a mixture of $\frac{1}{2}$ large bottle Teriyaki sauce and 6 oz. of pineapple juice. Take up from marinade and sprinkle with Lawry's seasoned salt. Cook on grill 15 to 17 minutes per side. Take off grill and place in center of heavy foil. Mix $\frac{1}{2}$ cup bourbon, $\frac{1}{3}$ to $\frac{1}{2}$ box brown sugar, 4 to 6 tablespoons honey and remaining marinade mixture. Pour over tenderloin and seal foil. Place back on grill for 20 minutes.

Chicken To Go Biscuits

MELANIE & SCOTT HOWARD
Scott is color announcer for Bulldog football
and play-by-play announcer for Georgia Basketball.

2 tbs. Butter or margarine
2 tbs. flour
$\frac{1}{4}$ tsp. salt
Dash pepper
$\frac{1}{2}$ cup milk
2 cups cubed cooked chicken
$1\frac{1}{4}$ shredded cheddar cheese
$\frac{1}{2}$ cup (4 oz.) chopped or sliced drained mushrooms
1 (1 lb. 0.3 oz.) can Pillsbury Grands refrigerated
    buttermilk biscuits
1 egg, slightly beaten
3 cups cornflakes, crushed

Heat oven to 375 degrees. In medium saucepan, melt butter, stir in flour, salt and pepper until well blended. Add milk all at once. Cook about 1 minute until thickened, stirring occasionally. Stir in chicken, cheese, mushrooms. Set aside.

Separate biscuit dough into eight biscuits. Roll or pat each into 5-inch circle. Place about $\frac{1}{3}$ cup chicken mixture on each biscuit circle. Wrap dough around chicken mixture, pressing edges to seal.

Dip rolls in egg, then coat with crushed cornflakes. Place on ungreased cookie sheet. Bake at 375 degrees for 20 to 25 minutes until golden brown. Four servings.

Julie Moran always had her sights set on network television and her first big break was with the NBA and NBC's "Inside Stuff." Then ABC hired her to work (sideline announcer) with Keith Jackson, another native Georgian who is still doing network play by play for ABC.

She grew up in Thomasville. Her mother, Barbara, was a beauty queen at Georgia and her father, Paul, lettered in baseball for Jim Whatley. Her grandfather was longtime Georgia coach and recruiter, Sterling DuPree. As a little girl and subsequently a precocious teenager, Julie would practice being an announcer and often interviewed her grandfather who critiqued her work. She loved her granddaddy and she loves Georgia. For years she was the weekend anchor for Entertainment Tonight but left a few months ago to do other things.

Back home in California, she is always checking scores to see how the Dogs did on Saturday.

"You can't imagine the pride I have when I learn that the Bulldogs have won a big game. That is important to me."

Chicken Brunswick Stew

JULIE & ROB MORAN

1 hen cooked and boned
1 16 oz. can cream style corn
1 16 oz. can tomatoes
1 large onion, chopped
1 8 oz. bottle chili sauce
2 tbs. Worcestershire sauce
¼ cup vinegar

1 tsp. dry mustard
½ stick butter
1 pint chicken broth (saved from the hen)
Salt and pepper to taste

Combine all ingredients. Simmer for 1½ hours. May be served over rice, or in a cup.

Chicken Mull

ANN & CHARLIE HORTON

6 chicken breasts
4 medium onions
1 quart milk
1 stick butter
1 box Saltine crackers
Salt and pepper to taste
Tabasco sauce
Worcestershire sauce
Red pepper

Skin chicken and cook over low heat until the meat falls off the bone. Remove from pot and cut into bite sized pieces. Add chopped onion to pot and simmer until tender. Add chicken and butter. Add Worcester sauce, pepper and red pepper and Tabasco to taste. Slowly add milk and crushed crackers to desired consistency. Continue to add seasonings to desired taste.

Blue Plate Steak

TINA & TOMMY TINKER

1½ lbs. ground beef
2 scallions, finely chopped
¼ cup seasoned breadcrumbs
1 egg
1 tablespoon yellow mustard
1 (12 oz.) jar beef gravy
½ cup water
2 teaspoons horseradish
½ lb. fresh mushrooms, sliced

In a medium bowl, combine the ground beef, scallions, breadcrumbs, egg, and mustard, mix well. Shape into four ½-inch-thick oval patties.

Coat a large skillet with nonstick cooking spray and preheat over medium-high heat. Place the patties in the skillet and cook for 3 to 4 minutes per side, or until no pink remains. Add the gravy, water, horseradish, and mushrooms and cook for 4 to 5 minutes, or until the mushrooms are tender, stirring occasionally. Serves 4.

Brats in Beer

BRAD & JILL ZIMANEK

Johnsonville bratwurst
Several cans of beer (any brand)
Onions
French sandwich rolls

This recipe can be done backwards or forwards and still taste the same – delicious! Boil brats in beer and onions (if precooked, until heated: if raw, for 20 minutes). Then grill, or grill brats ahead, then store in crock pot of heated beer and onions. Serve on soft French sandwich rolls. Top brats with your standard hotdog topping (cheese, relish, onions, pickles, tomatoes, mustard, ketchup). This is a standard Green Bay Packers tailgating meal.

Chicken Winglets

JoAn & TONY SALLOUM

16 chicken wings
2 tsp. butter
¾ cup bread crumbs
¾ cup parmesan cheese
1 tsp. dried basil
½ tsp. oregano

Wash wings and pat dry. Combine bread crumbs, cheese and seasonings in a large bowl and mix well. Melt butter. Dip each wing in butter, then in the crumb mixture. Arrange in a baking dish and bake at 375 degrees for 30 minutes or until lightly brown.

Charley Trippi has been a wonderful friend since he got back to Athens from an outstanding professional career with the old Chicago Cardinals. Charley often took me on recruiting trips, buying me a big, expense account steak. That was nice. He'd let me have a beer, too, if I wanted one, and most often I wanted one. I was afraid to ask for two.

Growing up in Pittston, Pa., Charley was discovered by a former Georgia player who ran Coca-Cola operations in Wilkes Barre. He told Charley that he had a scholarship to Georgia when he finished high school. After high school, Charley enrolled at LaSalle Military Academy. That is where he blossomed as a football player and colleges everywhere tried to sign him. Harold (War Eagle) Ketron knew Trippi was something special. He would often call Coach Butts at night, after he had been drinking something other than Coca-Cola.

"You gotta sign this boy, Wally," he would say. "He's the slickest back I have ever seen." One night Coach Butts needled Mr. Ketron, asking, "Just how slick is he?"

Ketron, who grew up in Clarkesville said, "Wally he is slicker than owl sh_t in the moonlight."

Charley's Chops
CHARLEY & PEGGY TRIPPI

6 pork chops (boneless center cut loin ½ inch or so)
6 medium potatoes
2 large onions (sweet is best)
½ cup Italian bread crumbs
½ cup grated parmesan cheese
1 egg
Salt and pepper to taste

Peel and cut potatoes into quarters. Brown lightly in small amount of oil. Place into lightly greased baking dish. Slice onions thinly – sauté until tender. Place onions on top of potatoes. Salt and pepper chops according to taste and dip each chop into egg, then dredge in mixture of cheese and crumbs. Brown chops in small amount of olive oil. Place chops on top of onions and potatoes. Bake in 325 degree oven about 45 to 60 minutes.

Chicken may be used instead of chops. Recipe may be prepared a day or two ahead of baking. It's still great. Men love it!

Never has there been a better neighbor than Agnew Peacock, who played high school football with Fran Tarkenton. An electrician by trade, he can fix anything. For years when we had a hint of a problem at our house, we put in a call to Agnew. Without doubt, he is the world's greatest neighbor. When he moved to another house, Myrna and I literally cried. I used to tell him that I cannot do anything with my hands like he can. Agnew would always counter, "but I can't type."

> *If I am as tenth as good at the keyboard as Agnew is with his tool box and power saw, then I am, at least, moderately successful.*
>
> *Agnew is a great American.*

Barbecue Venison on the Grill

AGNEW & HILDA PEACOCK

1 stick margarine
1 tablespoon minced onions
1 tablespoon black pepper
4 tablespoons brown sugar
4 tablespoons vinegar
4 tablespoons lemon juice
4 tablespoons sherry wine
1 large bottle A-1 steak sauce
1 large bottle Worcestershire sauce
1 jar red currant jelly

Trim and marinate back quarter of ham 24 hours in oil, Worcestershire sauce and lemon juice.

Cook on grill over low heat 3 to 4 hours. Continue to brush marinade over meat.

Mix together sauce and simmer over low heat for 30 minutes. Pour sauce over meat after it is prepared and sliced.

Barbecue Biscuits

DOLORES & NED HUGHES

Heat 3 to 4 tablespoons of butter. Put in 1½ lbs. of ground beef that has been sprinkled with flour and 1 cup finely chopped onions and brown together. Add the following ingredients.

1 cup tomato soup
¼ cup brown sugar
2 tablespoons vinegar
1½ tablespoons chili powder
2½ cups water

Cook over low heat. Spoon into buns when mixture is cooked thick. This is also very good over hot dogs or over spaghetti.

> When he worked at WSB television in Atlanta, Tom Brokaw brought his wife to Athens for the Georgia-Alabama game in 1965, the never-to-be forgotten battle in which the Bulldogs flee-flickered the Tide, 18-17. Brokaw had played high school football in South Dakota and says he has always been a football fan. He had heard about the enthusiasm for Southeastern Conference football but had not experienced competition up close.
>
> On his trip to Athens, he observed the enthusiasm and tailgating and the festive atmosphere, something he has always enjoyed about fall Saturday afternoons on a college campus. Georgia to him seemed special. I once interviewed him at NBC in New York about Georgia football.

From his experience in Athens for a game that Bulldog loyalists will never forget, he became something of a Bulldog fan and keeps up with the Dogs in the fall.

"Yeah I do," he says. I always watch them from week to week when they are on TV. Now, I have lots of loyalties, you see. I come from the midwest originally and went to the University of Iowa for a period of time, so I kind of have to keep an eye out for Iowa. I finished my education at a little tiny school called the University of South Dakota which has had good teams so I have to keep track of them. Then I lived in California for a spell and got very attached to UCLA and the great USC/UCLA rivalry. My daughter went to Stanford so I've got all these loyalties spread out across the country. Georgia is certainly one of them. I keep track of the Bulldogs, I keep track of the Hawkeyes, South Dakota the Stanford Cardinals and the UCLA Bruins. So, as my wife says, I can always come up with a winner.

With your background, do people find it unusual that you might have Georgia loyalty?

"They're always a little surprised when I say I lived in Atlanta and I have a real affection for the South, and a much keener appreciation, I think, for the South than if I had not lived there. I've always counted that as one of the important stops in my career because I think that the South remains a distinctive region in our country. It's changed, too, surely, but the fact of the matter is that everyone should have an opportunity to get to know the people there and to find out what institutions are important and how the culture functions and the

richness of the South. I've always counted that as a real blessing, having lived there and having been exposed to the Southern traditions."

That would, of course, include college football tailgating.

College football has never had a better friend that Keith Jackson who grew up in Carroll County. The settlement where he lived was Roopville.

He rode a mule named Pearl to school and listened to games on WSB radio. He was fond of the Bulldogs teams of the forties, and had a great appreciation for the play of Charley Trippi.

Keith is big time, but he still functions without a trace of ego or arrogance. And, he is a man of great loyalty, which is, in large part, why he continues to broadcast college games for ABC. He would be the first to say, even with all the problems out there today, college football remains the greatest of games.

When he was working a game in Sanford Stadium a few years ago, we did a pre-game radio show on the grounds on the east side of Field Street. I asked Keith to be a guest on the show before he moved into the stadium for his afternoon's work with ABC.

As the interview began, he leaned in and said, "I've always been anxious to do this," and then he said: "Welcome South Brother," which is the phrase from which WSB gets it call letters.

Here's a recipe from Keith, and his wife, Turi:

"We have never had time to do much tailgating since I have been going to the stadiums of the world early for work. Very seldom do we eat in the Press Box. Almost always we bring or order in our own food. There is a certain satisfaction to that and I guess you have to be in the media business to understand it.

"So this so-called menu for outdoor dining is basically designed for the back of the boat on fishing days and sometimes for surviving ferry traffic.

"Start the day with a fried egg sandwich...on whole wheat bread...one or two eggs flat fried. One or two pieces of back bacon or thinly sliced ham. Mayo or whatever to taste and if you want to give it a little pop add a slice of jalapeno jack cheese.

"Back it up with sliced cantaloupe sealed in a Ziploc bag. Cantaloupe keeps better than watermelon...but can do either or both in separate bags.

"Pepper cheese...boison is what we use with rice crackers...and Norwegian goat cheese on flat bread are great tasting and filling for snacks.

"And if there is a real demand for gusto...then another sandwich of any kind can be added. We like cold thinly sliced strip sirloin...horseradish and mustard on small slices of a sourdough baguette.

"Top it with some real plain water. Skipper can't drink wine on our boat and it makes him cranky if anybody else does."

DESSERTS

Sweets . . . but sweeter if the chapel bell rings.

Molasses Cookies

KEN & AMY (WHITTEMORE) HYATT

¾ cup butter flavored shortening
⅓ cup white sugar
⅔ cup brown sugar
1 egg
¼ cup grandma's molasses
2 cups flour
2 teaspoons baking soda
¼ teaspoon salt
½ teaspoon cloves
1 teaspoon ginger
1 teaspoon cinnamon
White raisins
Chopped pecans

Sift together flour, soda, salt, cloves, ginger, and cinnamon. Set aside.

Cream together shortening, sugars, egg and molasses. Add flour mixture and mix well.

Add raisins and nuts to taste. Bake at 350 degrees for eight minutes.

Grilled Apples

TINA & TOMMY TINKER

1 Granny Smith apple, cored
1 tablespoon brown sugar
¼ teaspoon ground cinnamon

Fill the core of the apple with the brown sugar and cinnamon. Wrap the apple in a large piece of heavy foil, twisting the extra foil into a tail for a handle. Place the apple in the coals of a campfire or barbeque and let cook 5 to 10 minutes, until softened. Remove and unwrap, being careful of the hot sugar. Serve with vanilla ice cream on the side.

Japanese Fruitcake

JOSEPH DABNEY

Filling

2 cups sugar
4 tbs. Flour
1½ cups boiling water
1 fresh coconut (grate fine)
2 lemons (grate fine)
2 oranges (grate fine)

Cake layers

1 cup butter
2 cups sugar
3 cups flour
4 tsp. baking powder
1 cup milk
6 eggs
1 cup pecans
3 tsp. cinnamon
1 box raisins
1 tsp. cloves
1 tsp. nutmeg

Filling

In a saucepan combine sugar and flour. Mix thoroughly. Add boiling water, then add grated coconut,

continued

lemon and oranges. Cook mixture on low for about 20 minutes, stirring constantly. Cook until mixture reaches proper consistency but not too runny. Set aside.

Cake batter

In a large bowl, mix butter and sugar in mixer until fluffy. Add flour, baking powder, milk and eggs (one at a time), and beat everything in as you go. Next add to batter pecans, cinnamon, raisins, cloves and nutmeg. Pour batter into cake pans and bake at 325 to 350 degrees. Bake until golden brown on top. When baked, punch tiny holes in each layer.

Final step

Put first layer down (with holes in it) on cake plate. Pour filing on top. Do same with second and third layers, then pour filling over the cake's top.

Glorified Brownies

NAN & BILL O'LEARY

Cream 1 stick of butter and 1 cup sugar – add 2 beaten eggs.
¾ cup flour
1 cup pecans, chopped (optional)
3 tbsp. cocoa
Pinch of salt

Bake at 350 degrees for 30 minutes in 8" x 8" pan. Take out of oven and push mini marshmallows into entire top of hot brownies. While cooling prepare icing.

Icing

2 cups sifted powdered sugar (10x)
½ stick butter
3 tbsp. Cocoa
4 tbsp. half and half

Beat until creamy. Spread on brownies.

Georgia Bulldog Apple Cake

MARGARET WALKER HUTCHESON

1½ cups cooking oil
2 cups sugar
4 eggs
3 cups sifted flour
1 teaspoon salt
1 teaspoon soda
2 teaspoons vanilla
3 large tart apples, cut into small pieces
1¾ cups chopped pecans

Combine cooking oil, sugar and eggs for 3 minutes at medium speed. Add flour sifted with salt and soda. Add vanilla and be sure entire mixture is blended well. Fold in chopped apples and nuts. Bake in tube cake pan, which is well greased and floured, for 1 hour and 20 minutes at 325 degrees. Cool 20 minutes and pour on the sauce while still hot.

Sauce

1 stick butter
2 tablespoons milk ½ cup light brown sugar firmly packed

In double boiler bring to a boil and cook 20 minutes. While still hot, pour on cake. It will be thin and will soak into cake.

> *Deborah Norville, Dalton native and host of Inside Edition, has great feelings for the University of Georgia. "I'm proud of my journalism degree from the University," she says.*
>
> *She is a star in television circles, but enjoys returning to her hometown of Dalton.*
>
> *When she was with NBC, she invited me to stand near her while she did the news. I was only a few feet away. I could have reached out and tapped her on the shoulder.*
>
> *The whole time, I was worried about sneezing or not being able to stifle a cough. After the newscast we went to her office and talked about Georgia and Athens for a column I was writing. I love interacting with Georgia graduates in high places. It is one of the fun things about my work. But I also like the so-called commoners. If you are a Bulldog, you are okay with me.*

Fresh Apple Cake
DEBORAH NORVILLE

2 cups sugar
3 cups flour
1 tsp. soda
1 tsp. salt
1 tsp. cinnamon
1½ cups Wesson oil
3 eggs

1 tsp. vanilla
3 cups chopped red apples (do not peel)
1 cup chopped nuts

Sift together dry ingredients; add oil, eggs, and vanilla. Stir in the apples and nuts. Grease (but do not flour) a tube pan. Bake at 350 degrees for 1 hour. Cool 10 minutes in pan and turn out on plate. Serve with sweetened whipped cream.

Peanut Sticks
MARJORIE & LEONARD COBB

1 long loaf of whole wheat bread (not 100% kind)

Remove crust and save. Cut each slice in 5 to 6 strips. Toast strips and crust and end pieces in 200 degree oven until dry and crusty, about 2 hours. Don't brown.

Crumbs

Crush or grind trimmings and ends and place in a bowl.

Mix

½ cup smooth peanut butter
½ cup vegetable oil
Blend with a wire whip until smooth and well blended.

Dip Strips (you can hold 2 or 3 at a time)

In mixture hold over mixture and let drain. Then roll strips in crushed crumb mixture. Place in container for storage. Stores well in tin cans (cookie or popcorn cans).

Pecan Praline Cake

WINKI & GENE MAC WINBURN

2 cups light brown sugar
½ cup butter (or margarine)
2 eggs
1 cup buttermilk
1 teaspoon soda
2 cups plain flour
2 heaping tablespoons cocoa
1 tablespoon vanilla

Warm buttermilk and butter. Put in mixing bowl. Add brown sugar and eggs and beat thoroughly. Add dry ingredients, sifted together. Mix well. Add vanilla. Bake in greased and floured rectangular pan, 2 inches deep, about 9" x 14". bake at 350 degrees for 20 to 25 minutes.

Icing

1 stick margarine
1 cup brown sugar
1 cup pecans, chopped
6 tablespoons light cream or top milk

Mix all ingredients. As soon as cake is done, spread mixture on top of cake. Turn oven to broil. Place cake on bottom and cook until icing bubbles and is light brown. This takes only a few minutes. Cut into squares and serve.

Dirt Pudding

TINA & TOMMY TINKER

1 large package Oreo cookies
1 large container Cool Whip
1 (8 oz.) package Philadelphia cream cheese
¼ cup margarine
1 cup powdered sugar
2 small packages instant French vanilla pudding
3 cups milk

Crumble ⅔ package cookies in 13" x 9" inch cake pan. Mix together Cool Whip, cream cheese, margarine and powdered sugar. In large bowl, mix together pudding and mild. Combine cream cheese mixture with pudding mixture; mix well; pour over cookies. Crumble remaining cookies on top.

Tailgate Turtle Bars

GLADA GUNNELLS & MICHAEL HORVAT

Melt one stick of margarine. Pour over 15 ounces of crushed vanilla wafers and press into the bottom of a Pyrex dish.

Spread one 12 ounce package of semisweet chocolate chips over the vanilla wafer layer.

Cover with one cup or more of chopped pecans.

Drizzle one 12¼ ounce jar of caramel topping over the other layers.

Bake for 15 minutes at 350 degrees.

Cool in refrigerator two hours before you take out and cut into squares.

Frank Ros was born in Spain. His father later moved the family to Greenville, S. C., where he attended high school and learned to play football. While at Georgia he and his teammates got in trouble for stealing a pig to roast at the conclusion of spring practice. They had to spend the summer painting the wall around the football practice field for their miscreant deed.

The team's notorious theft and cookout helped bring about a bonding that led to the National Championship of 1980.

Frank likes to cook out. His pretty wife, Jan, is an Auburn graduate and when Auburn and Georgia line up each year, Frank says, "she knows not to mess with me on that weekend."

Pumpkin Bars
WILLIAM RUBY

2 cups flour
2 teaspoons baking power
1 teaspoon baking soda
½ teaspoon salt
2 teaspoons cinnamon
2 cups sugar

Sift above together in mixing bowl. Then add 4 slightly beaten eggs, 2 cups pumpkin #303 can, 1 cup cooking oil, 1 cup nuts, if desired. Bake in moderate oven, 350 degrees in two 9" x 18" greased and floured pans about 25 minutes.

Southern Pound Cake
JAN & FRANK ROS

3 cups plain flour
3 cups sugar
½ cup Crisco
2 sticks butter (melted)
¾ teaspoon baking powder
2 teaspoons vanilla flavoring
5 eggs
1 cup milk

Cream together Crisco, butter and sugar. Sift flour and baking powder three times. Mix ingredients alternately with milk and eggs. Add vanilla flavoring last. Spray your bundt pan with Bakers Joy then pour the ingredients in and bake 90 minutes at 325 degrees.

Plum Pudding Cake
MARY & MIKE ADAMS

2 cups sugar
2 small jars Gerber plums with Tapioca
1 cup chopped nuts
less than 1 tbsp. cinnamon
2 cups self-rising flour
1 cup oil
4 eggs
½ tbsp. cloves

Mix all ingredients. Grease and flour tube pan. Bake at 350 degrees for 1 hour.

Peanut Brittle

MRS. RUBEN STRICKLAND (GERTRUDE)
(VIA HUBERT MOSELEY)

Prepare ahead
3 ½ cups raw peanuts
2 cups sugar
1 cup white corn syrup
¼ cup water
Dash salt
2 tsp. soda

Combine first 5 ingredients and bring to a boil. Cook until peanuts are light brown and mixture turns a golden color. Add soda, stir and pour on buttered cookie sheet. Pull as thin as possible. When cooled, break into pieces.

Date Nut Bars

SANDRA & BEN BELUE

1 ½ cups self-rising flour
2 cups sugar
1 cup Mazola oil
2 teaspoon vanilla
4 eggs
1 cup chopped dates
1 cup chopped pecans

Mix sugar, oil and eggs in large mixing bowl. Gradually add flour and then vanilla. Stir in dates and nuts by hand. Pour into greased 13" x 9" x 2" baking pan. Bake at 325 degrees for 45 minutes.

Crunch Cake

BECKY & LAMAR LEWIS

1 cup Crisco
2 cups sugar
2 cups cake flour
6 large eggs
½ teaspoon salt
1 tablespoon lemon juice
1 small bottle pure almond extract

Preheat oven to 325 degrees. Mix all ingredients together and beat at medium speed 10 minutes. Pour into greased and floured tube pan (not Teflon) and bake one hour. Cool in pan 10 minutes. Run knife around sides and center stem, invert and finish cooling. Freezes well.

This is truly a "crunch cake" in appearance…not a very pretty cake because of the crumbling. However, it is delicious by itself or as strawberry shortcake or topped with vanilla ice cream, chocolate syrup, whipped cream and a cherry on top.

Chocolate Chip Pie

SHANNON & ED FERGUSON

9 inch pie shell, uncooked
1 (6 oz.) package chocolate chips
1 stick melted butter
1 cup sugar
2 eggs well beaten
½ cup flour
1 teaspoon vanilla
1 cup chopped pecans (optional)

Pour chips in bottom of pie crust. Mix the rest of the ingredients and pour over chips. Bake at 325 to 350 degrees for 45 minutes.

Cobbler

BILL & NAN O'LEARY

Cut apples (mangos-whatever) in pieces. Fill a 9" x 13" pyrex dish with cut fruit. Sprinkle with cinnamon, ginger, allspice according to taste. Prepare topping.

Topping

2 cups sugar
1 cup self-rising flour
1 egg (beaten)
1 stick margarine or butter

Mix sugar, flour and beaten egg together. Sprinkle over fruit. Pour melted margarine over that. Bake at 350 degrees about 45 minutes to 1 hour until brown and fruit is fork tender.

Chocolate Macaroons

MARTHA TRAMMELL WYANT

1 stick butter
2 cups sugar
4 heaping tablespoons cocoa
1/2 cup milk

1 teaspoon vanilla
3 cups oatmeal (either kind)
1 cup chopped pecans

Bring butter, sugar, cocoa and milk to a boil. Stirring all the time. Boil 1 minute. Add vanilla and stir. Add oatmeal and nuts and stir well. Drop 1 tablespoon each on cookie sheet. Refrigerate. If mixture starts getting hard, set pan in hot water.

Chocolate Chip Pecan Cookies

MARTHA TRAMMELL WYANT

1 cup Crisco
1 cup brown sugar
1/2 cup white sugar
1 teaspoon vanilla
2 eggs
2 cups flour
1 teaspoon salt
1 teaspoon soda
2 cups chocolate chips, semi-sweet
2 cups toasted pecans

Combine Crisco, brown sugar and white sugar in mixer or food processor. Add vanilla and eggs. Combine flour, salt and soda then add to rest of the mixture. Process until it forms a dough. Remove from mixer to bowl and add chocolate chips and pecans. Put on cookie sheets and bake at 350 degrees for 9 to 11 minutes. Makes about 30 cookies

Chocolate Chip Cookies
LEONARD COBB

2¼ cups plain all purpose flour
1 teaspoon baking soda
1 teaspoon salt
1 cup (2 sticks) butter softened
¾ cup granulated sugar
¾ cup packed brown sugar
2 teaspoon vanilla flavoring pure extract
2 eggs
1 (12 oz.) package chocolate chips, semi-sweet
1 cup chopped pecans

Sift first 3 ingredients together in mixing bowl. In a large mixing bowl cream butter and sugar well and add vanilla. Add eggs one at a time, beat well after each. Fold dry ingredients into creamed mixture until mixed. Add 2 tablespoons of water, stir in chocolate chips and nuts. I like to chill mixture several hours or overnight.

Preheat oven to 375 degrees. Use #70 scoop or rounded teaspoon and shave into small balls. Place on ungreased cookie sheet, press down slightly. Bake 9 to 11 minutes until golden brown. Let sit 2 minutes then remove with spatula to wire rack.

John Donaldson played at Georgia and coached for the Bulldogs. The only blemish on his Bulldog record is that he likes Steve Spurrier whom he coached as a freshman when John was on the Florida coaching staff. But he always wanted Georgia to beat Spurrier. "We just weren't competitive with a couple of coaching

staffs, and it burned the hell out of me," John says.

He loves Georgia but win or lose, he'll go fishing. He has a wonderful coastal home at Shellman Bluff and every day, weather encouraging and tides right, he heads into the marsh.

I remember one outing when I saw his line spin off his reel, having hooked something too big and strong for his lightweight equipment. A 26-pound spot tail bass had taken his bait and only finesse would bring the quarry home. Only skill would succeed. Power and force would lose this battle. Tiring out his prey with the velvet touch, gained him the catch of the fall.

I had just seen man and nature in perfect harmony.

Caramel Brownies
ANNE & JOHN DONALDSON

2 cups brown sugar
⅓ lb. Shortening, butter or margarine
1¼ cup plain flour
2 eggs
1 cup nuts
1 tsp. Vanilla

Cream shortening. Add sugar, eggs. Put in 13" x 9½" x 2½" pan. Bake at 325 degrees for 20 minutes. Don't overcook! Cut in squares. Roll in powdered sugar (optional).

Chocolate Torte
BARBARA & VINCE DOOLEY

1 stick oleo
1 cup sifted flour
½ cup chopped nuts

Spread over bottom of pan (7" x 11"). Cook 15 minutes at 375 degrees then cool.

Mix

8 oz. cream cheese
1 cup Confectioners sugar
1 cup Cool Whip

Spread over cooled crust.
   Mix 1 package instant Chocolate pudding with 1½ cups cold milk. Spread over other two layers.
   Spread Cool Whip over the top.

Apple Pie Filling
TINA & TOMMY TINKER

Spread the filling in a small roasting pan or casserole dish. Mix up a regular cake mix (spice is very good with apple). Pour on top of the pie filling. Bake as usual, 350 degrees for 30 or 40 minutes. When cool, cut slices and with a server or spatula pick up a slice and turn over on plate as you would a pineapple upside down cake. Better to heat before serving. You can use any combination, cherry pie filling with white or cherry chip cake mix, etc.

> *Trisha Yearwood, the country singer, attended Georgia briefly, and my ambition is to get her to Sanford Stadium to sing "Georgia On My Mind," to a packed house. I'm working on it.*

Brownies
TRISHA YEARWOOD

2 squares unsweetened chocolate
⅓ cup solid shortening
1 cup sugar
2 well beaten eggs
⅔ cup plain flour
½ teaspoon baking powder
½ teaspoon salt
1 cup chopped pecans
1 teaspoon vanilla extract

Melt chocolate and shortening together. Add the sugar to the well beaten eggs; combine the mixtures. Sift flour, measure; add baking powder and salt; sift again. Add the dry ingredients to the egg mixture; add nuts and vanilla. Spread the dough evenly in a greased square pan, 8" x 8" x 2" inches. Bake at 350 degrees for 25 to 30 minutes.
   When cool cut into squares or bars.
   Note: Trisha usually doubles this recipe and bakes in a 9" x 13" pan, increasing the baking time as necessary. These brownies do not need frosting as they develop a wonderful crunchy crust as they bake. They keep will if there are ever any left. They are a band favorite!

Brownie Cake

BETTY FOY & CARL SANDERS

Carl is former governor and has always been happy to look after the university.

1 cup water
2 sticks butter
2 cups sugar
2 cups plain flour, sifted
$\frac{1}{2}$ teaspoon salt
1 teaspoon soda
4 tablespoons of cocoa
$\frac{1}{2}$ cup buttermilk
2 eggs, beaten
1 teaspoon vanilla

Icing

1 teaspoon vanilla
1 stick butter, melted
6 tablespoons canned milk (Carnation)
1 box 4X confection sugar
4 tablespoons cocoa
1 cup chopped pecans

Boil the water and butter together. Add the sugar, flour, salt, soda and cocoa to boiled butter water. Add the buttermilk, eggs and vanilla. Spray 9" x 11" Pyrex with Baker's Joy and bake at 325 degrees for 25 minutes. Spread icing on cake while its warm. Stay moist. Cut in squares. Serves 12.

Brownies

KERRI & DAMON EVANS

$\frac{1}{2}$ cup butter
2 squares chocolate, unsweetened
1 cup sugar
2 eggs
1 teaspoon vanilla
$\frac{3}{4}$ cup flour
$\frac{1}{2}$ cup nuts
Handful chocolate chips

Melt butter and chocolate in large bowl in microwave. Add sugar, then eggs and vanilla, mix well. Add flour, nuts and chocolate chips, mixing after each. Bake at 350 degrees for 30 minutes.

Aloha Bowl Coconut Cake

MARILOU & MATT BRASWELL

Marilou, former cheerleader, is the Bulldogs' cheerleading advisor and coach.

1 box white cake mix
2 pkg. Frozen coconut
8 oz. sour cream
1 $\frac{1}{2}$ cups sugar
Cream of coconut (one small can)
1 $\frac{1}{2}$ cups cool whip

Make layers and cut in half. Mix sugar, sour cream; add $\frac{3}{4}$ of coconut. Mix well. Place filling between layers. Mix remaining coconut and cool whip and top cake with mixture. Keep refrigerated. Aloha!

Bourbon Brownies

BONNIE & TRUETT JARRARD

1 (19.8 oz.) package family size fudge brownie mix
3 eggs
⅓ cup oil
1 cup chopped walnuts
6 tablespoons bourbon
½ cup softened butter
2 cups confectioner's sugar
3 tablespoons rum
6 oz. semisweet chocolate
4 tablespoons butter

Preheat oven to 350 degrees. Omitting the water called for on the package, combine brownie mix, eggs, oil and walnuts. Bake according package directions in a 9" x 13" inch pan. Remove from oven and immediately sprinkle with bourbon. Cool thoroughly. Combine butter, confectioner's sugar and rum. Spread evenly over brownies. Chill one hour. Melt chocolate and butter. Drizzle over brownies. Chill an additional hour or until chocolate hardens. With a warm knife, cut into 1 inch squares.

Miss Sarch's Pralines

NANCY & GARY COUVILLON

1 cup white sugar
1 cup light brown sugar
2 tbs. white Karo syrup
2 tbs. butter
Pinch of salt
½ cup evaporated milk

Mix together in heavy saucepan. Bring to boil and cook until it reaches 237 degrees on candy thermometer. Remove from heat and add 2 cups pecan halves and 1 teaspoon vanilla.

Beat until it thickens. Spoon out about 2 to 3 tablespoons at a time on wax paper and let cool. Makes approximately 18 to 20.

Mocha Polka Walnut Torte

BUBBER & NANCY SCRUGGS

1 (16 oz.) package brownie mix
2 eggs
¼ cup water
½ cup coarsely chopped walnuts
2 cups whipping cream
½ cup brown sugar, firmly packed
2 tablespoons instant coffee
Walnut halves

Follow cake method for brownies on package: that is, stir in eggs and water into brownie mix, then add walnuts (pecans may be used instead). Spoon into two greased 8-inch layer bake pans. Bake at 350 degrees at 20 minutes. Turn out immediately on racks to cool.

Whip cream until it begins to thicken. Gradually add brown sugar and instant coffee. Continue beating until of spreading consistency. Spread between layers of torte and swirl over top and sides of torte. Polka dot with walnut halves. Chill overnight before serving. Very rich so cut in fairly small slices. Makes 15 to 16 Servings.

Mini Cheesecakes

SUE & BOB MARION

3 (8 oz.) packages soft cream cheese
5 eggs
1 cup sugar
½ tablespoon almond
1 ½ tablespoon vanilla

Cream cheese and sugar. Add eggs one at a time. Add flavorings. Fill smallest paper muffin cups ¾ full. Bake at 300 degrees for 20 to 25 minutes. Makes 36 to 40 cakes.

Mickey Gilley's Mississippi Apple Cake

MICHELE CLOVIS

1 cup sugar
1 stick margarine
2 eggs
1 ¼ tsp. soda
1 tbsp. cinnamon
1 ½ cups plain flour
1 cup buttermilk
3 raw apples, chopped

Cream sugar and margarine. Add eggs and beat well. Sift soda and cinnamon with flour. Add flour and milk to creamed mixture. Last add apples by folding. Bake in a greased tube pan at 325 degrees for 50 to 60 minutes.

Topping

½ cup cream
½ tsp. vanilla
1 cup grated coconut
3 tbsp. margarine
⅔ cup light brown sugar
½ cup chopped pecans

Cream sugar and margarine. Add cream, vanilla, coconut and pecans. Spread over cake. Return to oven until sugar has melted.

Tom Johnson, late of CNN, was a classmate at Georgia. He married Edwina Chastain of Athens. She was in our wedding. We have visited with the Johnsons in Dallas, Los Angeles and wherever they have lived. But the best experience for me was visiting him when he was on the LBJ staff in Washington. He took me to lunch at the White House dining room and gave me a tour of the facilities including the Oval Office. When I left the White House, I was pleased that an old friend and classmate had risen so high so quickly. He never stayed out of touch with his alma mater and recently gave a six-figure check to the Bulldog baseball program. Coach David Perno, by the way, is married to Tom and Edwina's niece, the former Melanie Chastain of Athens.

Aunt Jo's Pound Cake

EDWINA & TOM JOHNSON

½ cup butter
½ cup Crisco
Add 3 cups sugar
6 eggs (one at a time)
1 teaspoon each of coconut, rum and almond extract
(or flavoring)
3 cups flour
1½ teaspoon baking powder
½ teaspoon salt
1 cup milk

Bake at 325 degrees for 1 hour 15 minutes to 1½ hours.

1 cup sugar
½ cup water
1 teaspoon of each above extracts

As soon as you remove from oven, make this glaze, bring to a boil and spoon over hot cake.

SPIRITS

A real tailgate scene!

Moonshine
RANDY BURNETTE

5 gallons water
5 lbs. sugar, stir until dissolved
5 lbs. plain cornmeal
1 package brewer's yeast or 4 to 5 tablets

Put in churn until it quits working, about 3 days.
Run through still slowly.

Eggnog
REMER & SUSAN LANE

2 dozen eggs, separated and whipped
4 quarts sugar
1 quart whipped cream
½ gallon vanilla ice cream
1/5 bourbon
4 oz. Meyers rum

Separate egg whites and yolks. Whip whites, add during whipping; set aside. Whip cream; set aside. Beat yolks. Add bourbon and rum while beating yolks. Add ice cream and continue beating. Add whipped cream and continue to beat slowly until smooth.
Makes 2½ gallons.

Wine Cooler
NANCY COUVILLON

2 cups orange juice
1 cup orange liqueur
6 oz. Frozen lemonade
1 Fifth white wine
28 oz. Carbonated water

Mix first four ingredients together. Right before serving add carbonated water.

Fitzyworld invented the following drink while tending bar at Cleve's on Baxter Street during Coach Dooley's and Coach Durham's best years. Many Athens natives dropped by Cleve's on a regular basis to have this drink:

Jo Mama Jo Daddy Jo Baby with a teetee-faced poopananny

White crème de cocoa
Crème de banana
Kahlua
Smattering of pineapple juice
Smattering of orange juice
Half and half

Using equal portions of each ingredient, add ice and tumble. Strain into shot glasses. Serves approximately 8 shooters.

Tiddlies (or alcoholic slushy)
JOY & TERRY WINGFIELD

½ gallon Blue Bell coffee ice cream
cheap Brandy
créam de coco

Let ice cream soften. Add créam de coco, brandy, and stir. Mix quantity to your preference.

Bloody Mary
HART & SHOOTER ROBERTS

1 quart Clamato juice
6 oz. vodka
8 dashes Dr. Tillitsuits or Worcestershire Sauce
2 heaping teaspoons prepared horseradish
Juice of 3 lemons
3 shakes of celery salt

Stir all ingredients together and pour over ice. Sprinkle with McCormick lemon and herb seasoning. Add a lime wedge.

This recipe makes a batch of Bloody Marys that will serve 4 to 6 people.

Coffee Delight
COURTNEY & PERRY JEWELL

Baileys Irish Cream
Starbucks breakfast blend coffee

Pour equal amounts of Irish cream and coffee over ice. For those who are continuing to party, use coffee with caffeine.

Tequila Sunrise
CLAIRE & JIM FORD

2 cans lime aid (thawed)
2 lime aid cans of water
1 beer
Tequila
3 tablespoons sugar

Empty the lime aid into your container. Mix one lime aid can of beer, 1½ lime aid cans of tequila and 3 tablespoons of sugar and pour into your lime aid. Stir and pour over ice.

Tailgate Chilled Beer a la Bat

GORDON VARNEDOE

*1 large cooler (large enough to contain enough
    servings for expected guest and some extra for
    the inevitable unexpected guests)*
Crushed or cubed ice
Water (amount equal to size of cooler)

Before serving follow these steps in sequence:
1. Place beer in cooler
2. Add ice generously
3. Add water to cover beer and ice entirely
4. Allow contents to sit undisturbed for eight (8, see recipe history) minutes. Serve chilled. For best results, serve with cozies.

Recipe History: While a student at Bulldog University, Gordon "Bat" Varnedoe and several colleagues of like mind performed extensive methods of getting beer from room temperature to chilled and drinkable temperature. This recipe is the result of lengthy serious testing. Enjoy.

The Dawg Shooter

DEMARIS & RAY TURK

1 oz. Macallan scotch
2 ice cubes

Mix together and drink. This recipe can be increased as needed per tailgaters.

Jack and Coke
The breakfast of champions

SVEIN & KATHARINE ROMSTAD

1 can Coca-Cola
Jack Daniel's bourbon

Generous portion of bourbon (subject to personal taste) Stirred, not shaken

Jan's Juice

JAN & STUART SATTERFIELD

Vodka
Orange juice
Fresca
Cranberry juice
Fresh-squeezed lemon

Mix accordingly to your desired taste. Serve over ice. This is a really great drink to serve in hot weather.

The Morning After
WENDELL & KIM PERRY

1 can V-8 juice
1 bottle Bud Lite beer

Mix together half V-8 juice and half beer. This drink is a "hang-over cure"!

The Wild, Wild West
RACHEL NORMAN

12 lemons
1 cup sugar
vodka
30 ice cubes

Put ice cubes in a container. Squeeze lemons over ice, add sugar and one cup of vodka. Let sit for 30 minutes, stirring occasionally. Pour in glass and serve.

Planter's Punch
PATRICIA & VERNON BRINSON

1 large can pineapple juice
1 small can frozen limeade
1 bottle (750 mL) of Myer's dark rum
1 healthy dollop of grenadine syrup

Pour all of the above ingredients into a gallon milk jug. Top with orange juice and shake well. Refrigerate. Better to serve the second day.

HOT & SPICY

More than likely, anybody who has spent time in a kitchen or who enjoys a spicy meal, has surely heard of Tabasco® sauce. Some eat Tabasco® with every meal.

Originated and still produced by the McIlhenny family from Avery Island, La., Tabasco® sells worldwide. You can get it in China, Russia and India. Europeans are big on Tabasco®, just like so many Americans we all know.

There is a Georgia connection with the McIlhenny family. Rosemary Dinkins is the daughter of Paul C.P. McIlhenny, and she is a Georgia graduate.

During her days on the Georgia campus, her father came to Athens a few times and cooked for her and her friends.

Cajun Chicken Burgers

1 pound fresh ground chicken or turkey
1 small onion, finely chopped
¼ cup chopped bell pepper
I clove garlic, minced
½ teaspoon Tabasco® brand Pepper Sauce
3 scallions, minced
I teaspoon Worcestershire sauce
Ground pepper

Combine all ingredients in medium bowl. Form into 4-inch patties. Broil or grill each side 4 to 6 minutes, depending on degree of desired doneness. Serve immediately. Makes 5 servings.

Santa Fe Chicken Wings

¼ cup lime juice
¼ cup vegetable oil
2 teaspoons Tabasco® brand Pepper Sauce
2 pounds chicken wings
2 tablespoons margarine
½ cup blue cornmeal
2 tablespoons flour
½ teaspoon salt
½ teaspoon ground cumin
⅛ teaspoon pepper

Mix lime juice, oil and Tabasco® Sauce in large bowl.

Cut each chicken wing at joints to make 3 pieces; discard tip. Cut off and discard excess skin. Place wings in oil mixture; stir to coat. Cover and refrigerate at least 3 hours, stirring occasionally; drain.

Heat oven to 425°F.

Heat margarine in 13" x 9" pan in oven until melted. Shake remaining ingredients in plastic bag or mix in bowl. Coat wings with cornmeal mixture; place in pan.

Bake 20 minutes uncovered. Turn chicken and bake 20 to 25 minutes longer until golden brown.

Makes 20 appetizers.

Chicken and Sausage Jambalaya

4 tablespoons vegetable oil
1 pound andouille or hot smoked sausage, cut into
 ½-inch slices
1 cup sliced celery
1 large onion, chopped
2 green or red bell peppers, chopped
2 cloves garlic, minced
3 cups chicken broth
1 can (16 ounces) whole peeled tomatoes, coarsely
chopped, undrained
2 bay leaves
1 teaspoon Tabasco® brand Pepper Sauce
½ teaspoon dried oregano leaves
½ teaspoon dried thyme leaves
¼ teaspoon ground allspice
1½ cups uncooked rice
1 pound cooked chicken, cubed into l-inch pieces
Celery leaves

Heat oil over medium-high heat in large heavy sauce-pot or Dutch oven. Add sausage, celery, onion, bell peppers and garlic. Cook 5 minutes or until vegetables are tender; stir frequently.

Stir in broth, tomatoes, bay leaves, Tabasco® Sauce, oregano, thyme and allspice. Bring to a boil. Reduce heat and simmer, uncovered, 10 minutes; stirring occasionally. Stir in rice. Cover; simmer 15 minutes. Add chicken; cover and simmer 5 minutes longer or until rice is tender.

Let stand covered 10 minutes. Remove bay leaf. Garnish with celery leaves. Makes 8 to l0 servings.

Nutritional information per serving: 513 calories, 30g protein, 35g carbohydrate, 27g fat, 88mg cholesterol, 1125mg sodium.

Spicy Chicken Wings

8 large chicken wings
¼ cup Tabasco® green pepper sauce
1 tablespoon Tabasco® pepper sauce
1 tablespoon Worcestershire Sauce
¾ teaspoon salt

Cut chicken wings at joint; discard wing tips. In medium bowl, combine pepper sauces, Worcestershire sauce and salt. Reserve 1 tablespoon mixture to brush over chicken later. Toss chicken pieces in mixture.

Preheat oven to 400°F. Arrange chicken in large baking pan. Cook 30 to 40 minutes until chicken is tender, brushing occasionally with sauce and turning occasinally. Just before serving, brush with reserved jalapeño mixture. Serve with Creamy Jalapeño Sauce.

Serves 4 as appetizers.

Buffalo Chicken Wings

Dip

½ cup sour cream
½ cup mayonnaise
2 teaspoons white wine vinegar
1 tablespoon chopped fresh parsley
1 tablespoon chopped green onion
½ teaspoon minced garlic
½ teaspoon Tabasco® brand Pepper Sauce
3 tablespoons crumbled blue cheese
Salt and pepper to taste

Chicken Wings

12 chicken wings
Vegetable oil for frying
4 tablespoons melted butter or margarine
1 teaspoon ketchup
2 teaspoons Tabasco® brand Pepper Sauce

Beat all dip ingredients together in small bowl until blended. Set aside.

Remove tips from wings and discard. Separate first and second joints of wings with sharp knife. Pat wings dry with paper towels. Heat 2 inches of oil in heavy saucepan to 350°F on deep-frying thermometer. Fry wings, a few at a time, for 6 minutes, until golden on all sides. Drain on paper towels.

Mix butter, ketchup and Tabasco® Sauce in small bowl. Toss wings in butter mixture to coat thoroughly. Serve hot and pass dip. Makes 24 pieces.

Hot wings, cool sauce, make a great combination!

Chargin' Chicken Drumsticks

½ cup butter or margarine (1 stick)
2 tablespoons Tabasco® brand Pepper Sauce
1 tablespoon ketchup
1 teaspoon salt
16 chicken drumsticks (about 4 pounds)
1 cup bottled blue cheese dressing

Preheat broiler.

Melt butter over low heat in small saucepan; stir in Tabasco® Sauce, ketchup and salt.

Place chicken drumsticks on rack in broiling pan; brush with some Tabasco® mixture. Broil chicken drumsticks 10 minutes 7 to 9 inches from heat source.

Turn and brush with remaining Tabasco® mixture. Broil 10 to 15 minutes longer or until drumsticks are browned and tender. Serve with blue cheese dressing.

Makes 8 servings.

Spicy Turkey Burgers

1 pound ground turkey
¼ cup grated onion
2 tablespoons plain yogurt
1 tablespoon fresh chopped dill or 1 teaspoon dried dill
1 large garlic clove, crushed
1½ teaspoons Tabasco® pepper sauce
1 teaspoon salt
4 Kaiser rolls, split
Lettuce leaves and tomato slices, optional

Preheat broiler or grill. Meanwhile, in large bowl combine ground turkey, onion, yogurt, dill, garlic, Tabasco sauce and salt and mix well. Shape mixture into four ½-inch-thick patties.

Broil or grill burgers 4 to 6 inches from heat source, 3 to 4 minutes on each side or until no longer pink inside.

To serve, place turkey burgers on rolls; top with lettuce and tomato slices.

Makes 4 servings.

Nutritional information per serving: 365 Calories, 26g protein, 14g fat, 982mg sodium, 57mg cholesterol.

Touchdown Cheese Scones

2 cups all-purpose flour
2 1/2 teaspoons baking powder
1/2 teaspoon baking soda
1/4 teaspoon salt
2 tablespoons cold butter or margarine, cut in pieces
1 cup grated mild cheddar cheese
2/3 cup buttermilk
2 large eggs, divided
1/4 teaspoon Tabasco® pepper sauce

Preheat oven to 350˚F. In large bowl, sift together flour, baking powder, baking soda and salt. Cut in butter until mixture resembles cornmeal. Stir in cheese. In small bowl, beat buttermilk, 1 egg and Tabasco sauce together. Make well in center of dry ingredients; add buttermilk mixture. Stir quickly and lightly with fork to form sticky dough. Turn dough out on lightly floured board. Knead gently 10 times. Divide dough in half; pat each half into circle about 1/2-inch thick. Cut each circle into 4 wedges. Combine remaining egg and 1 tablespoon water. Brush each wedge with egg mixture. Arrange on greased baking sheet. Bake 13 to 15 minutes or until golden.

Makes 8 scones.

Nutritional information per serving: 225 Calories, 9g protein, 9g fat, 92mg cholesterol, 385mg sodium.

Hot & Spicy Chex® Party Mix

1/4 cup margarine or butter, melted
1 tablespoon Lea & Perrins Worcestershire sauce
2 or 3 teaspoons Tabasco® brand Pepper Sauce
1 1/4 teaspoons Lawry's® seasoned salt
8 cups of your favorite Chex® brand cereals (corn, rice and/or wheat)
1 cup mixed nuts
1 cup pretzels
1 cup bite-size cheese crackers

Microwave Oven

Combine margarine, Worcestershire sauce, Tabasco® Sauce and seasoned salt; mix well. Pour cereals, nuts, pretzels and cheese crackers into large Glad-Lock® Zipper Bag.

Pour margarine mixture over cereal mixture inside Zipper Bag. Seal top of bag securely. Shake bag until all pieces are evenly coated.

Pour contents of bag into large microwave-safe bowl. Microwave on high 5 to 6 minutes, stirring throroughly every 2 minutes. While stirring, make sure to scrape sides and bottom of bowl. Spread on absorbent paper to cool. Store in airtight container.

Conventional Oven

Preheat oven to 250˚F. Follow steps 1 and 2 above.

Pour contents of bag into open roasting pan. Bake 1 hour, stirring every 15 minutes. Cool and store as directed above. Makes 11 cups.

Note: Due to differences in microwave ovens, cooking time may need adjustment. These directions were developed using 625 to 700 watt ovens.

Nutritional information per serving: 242 Calories, 5g protein, 29g carbohydrate, 12g fat, 1mg cholesterol, 655mg sodium.

Tangy Sangria

1 bottle red wine (750 ml)
2 ounces brandy
2 ounces triple sec
2 teaspoons fresh lime juice
2 teaspoons fresh orange juice
2 teaspoons sugar
½ teaspoon Tabasco® brand Pepper Sauce
½ orange, thinly sliced
½ lemon, thinly sliced
1 16-ounce bottle sparkling water

Combine red wine, brandy, triple sec, lime juice, orange juice, sugar, Tabasco® Sauce and fruit slices in a pitcher. Chill.

To serve, fill large wine glass with ice. Pour ⅔ full with sangría and top with sparkling water. Makes 6 to 8 servings.

Spicy Passion Punch (nonalcoholic)

2 cups orange-passion-kiwi juice
1 cup frozen raspberries, partially thawed
2 teaspoons Tabasco® brand Pepper Sauce
1 liter seltzer, chilled

Blend orange-passion-kiwi juice and raspberries in blender or food processor until smooth; stir in Tabasco® Sauce. Just before serving, stir in seltzer.

Makes 8 servings.

Millennium Mary

1 quart V8® 100% Vegetable Juice
1 cup vodka
1 tablespoon Worcestershire Sauce
1 tablespoon fresh lime juice
1 teaspoon Tabasco® brand Pepper Sauce
Lime wedges
Celery stalks

Combine all ingredients in 2-quart pitcher; stir well. Serve over ice. Garnish with lime wedges and celery stalks.

Makes 6 (6-ounce) servings.

Melon Cooler

4 cups honeydew melon chunks
2 tablespoons lime juice
1 tablespoon Tabasco® brand Green Pepper Sauce
½ cup vodka

Blend honeydew melon, lime juice and Tabasco® Sauce in blender or food processor until smooth. Stir in vodka. Refrigerate mixture until chilled.

Makes 2 servings.

* For a nonalcoholic drink, omit vodka.

MRS. SMITH'S RECIPE FILES

One day in late summer, I was visiting with my parents who live north of Wrightsville on Highway 57 in Central Georgia, not too far from the Oconee River.

While thumbing through an old magazine, I discovered an assortment of recipes my mother had collected over the years. They were not of the tailgate variety, but we are including them nonetheless.

Growing up, I, like most kids, seemed to always be hungry. Mealtime at our house was very tasty and filling. In the late spring and summer there were vegetables for every meal except breakfast. After developing a lasting taste for peas, I still get mouth watering palpitations when I am served peas at any meal.

In the spring and summer, when I am in town, I arise early on Saturday morning and head up to the two street markets in Athens. If the growers who set out their foodstuffs have peas and butterbeans, I often say to them, "I'll take all you got."

Then, I head home and start shelling. I grew up shelling peas and butterbeans, so I haven't forgotten how. This past summer, I met a nice gentleman named Jerry Thompson who has a sheller. Made friends with him right quick. I'll buy peas anywhere I find them and head out to Jerry's place in Vesta community, near Carlton. Putting vegetables in the freezer in summer makes the winter a season to enjoy.

My father and mother, James and Beatrice Smith, put up vegetables as far back as I can remember. Before freezers came about, vegetables were canned or put in those handy mason jars, which required a lot more work.

We take so much for granted now. We simply take our garden foods off the grocery chain shelves or out of those coolers. Simple and easy. No planting. No harvesting. No shelling or preparation. Just grab what you want, sack it up and cart it to the car. I maintain that for folks like me, those who don't have a garden, vegetables taste better when you at least have a hand in shelling, blanching and placing them in the freezer.

At any rate, I'll always appreciate the efforts of my parents, planting and harvesting and sharing with me and my brother and sisters.

Even now when I go home, I reminisce with them about the past when our garden meant that there would always be something to eat and enjoy when the temperatures dipped in winter.

Basic Pepperoni Pizza

Vegetable Spray
1 (12-inch) ready to bake pizza crust
½ to ¾ cup pizza sauce (more sauce may be added,
if desired)
2 cups (16-oz.) mozzarella cheese, shredded
and divided equally three times
1 (8 oz.) package Pepperoni
Italian seasonings

Preheat oven to 400 degrees. Spray round pizza pan with vegetable spray. Place pizza crust on pan. Top crust with pizza sauce, spreading evenly. Add a layer of mozzarella cheese, then a layer of pepperoni, sprinkle with Italian seasonings. Top with a final layer of mozzarella cheese. Bake 400 degrees for 10 to15 minutes or until cheese is melted and pizza is hot. Cut into slices and serve hot. Yields 1 pizza or 10 (4 oz) slices.

Carrot Pasta Salad

1 (12 oz) box tri-colored pasta, cooked according to
package directions, rinsed and drained well
4 medium carrots, thinly sliced
3 small Roma tomatoes, thinly sliced
1 medium green pepper, thinly sliced
1 cup Italian dressing
Salt and pepper

In a large bowl, add cooked pasta.

In a small bowl, combine vegetables and dressing. Microwave on high for 1 to 2 minutes or until vegetables are tender, but not mushy. Remove vegetables and allow them to cool. Add vegetables to the pasta and toss well. Cover and refrigerate overnight. Before serving, toss well; add salt and pepper to taste.
Yields 15 (4 oz) servings.

Bath salts recipe

You'll need a large bowl, small mixing cup, Epsom salts, glycerin, food coloring and perfume.

Measure 3 cups of Epsom salts into bowl. In the mixing cup, combine 1 tablespoon of glycerin, a couple drops of food coloring and some of your favorite perfume. Mix well. Slowly add this liquid mixture to the Epsom salts, stirring until mixed.

You now have a pretty and fragrant bath salts to enjoy. Be sure to store in a sealed container like a large mayo or pickle jar. You can even tie a fancy ribbon around it.

Hush Puppies

2 cups Dunn's Best Corn Meal
1 tablespoon flour
1 teaspoon soda
1 teaspoon baking powder
1 tablespoon salt
1 egg
6 tablespoons chopped onion
1 ½ to 2 cups buttermilk

Mix all dry ingredients, add chopped onion, then milk and egg. Drop by spoonful into deep hot grease where fish are cooking. Drain on paper towels.

Cornbread Salad

LYNN LAMB, STATESBORO, GA

1 (6 ounce) box cornbread mix
1 (12-ounce) package bacon
½ cup sweet pickle relish
½ cup sweet pickle juice
3 large tomatoes, chopped
1 large bell pepper, chopped
1 large Vidalia onion, chopped
1 cup mayonnaise or to taste

Prepare cornbread according to package directions. Cook; crumble into very small pieces. Cook bacon, drain and crumble or chop.

In large glass bowl, layer half of cornbread, top with half or pickle relish, juice, tomatoes, pepper, onion, bacon and ½ cup mayonnaise. Repeat layers, reserving small amount of tomatoes and bacon for garnish. Refrigerate; serve chilled. Yields 12 servings.

Note: All ingredients can be mixed together rather than layered, if desired.

Georgia Apple Cake

GEORGIA APPLE COMMISSION

3 cups all-purpose flour
1½ teaspoons baking soda
½ teaspoon salt
1 teaspoon cinnamon
2 eggs
2 cups sugar
1¼ cups vegetable oil

2 teaspoons vanilla extract
5 cups uncooked peeled chopped apples
1 cup chopped pecans

Sift together twice, the flour, baking soda, salt and cinnamon. In a separate bowl, beat eggs and sugar until creamy; add oil and vanilla, beat until smooth. Add dry ingredients and mix until a stiff dough forms. Stir in apples and pecans. Pour into greased and floured 10-inch tube pan. Bake at 350 degrees for 1 hour to 1 hour and 10 minutes or until brown. Yields 16 servings.

Georgia Peach Pound Cake

1 cup plus 2 tablespoons butter
2¼ cups sugar, divided
4 eggs
1 teaspoon vanilla
3 cups all-purpose flour, divided
1 teaspoon baking powder
½ teaspoon salt
2 cups chopped, fresh Georgia peaches

Grease a 10-inch tube pan with 2 tablespoons butter. Sprinkle pan with ¼ cup sugar. Cream remaining butter; gradually add remaining sugar, beating well. Add eggs, one at a time, beating well after each addition. Add vanilla and mix well. Combine 2¾ cups flour, baking powder, and salt; gradually add to creamed mixture, beating until well blended. Dredge peaches with remaining ¼ cup flour. Fold peaches into batter. Pour batter into prepared pan. Bake 325 degrees for 1 hour 10 minutes. Remove from pan and cool completely. Yield: 16 servings.

Georgia Caviar

KATHY HAYNES, ELBERTON, GA

1 pound dried black-eyed peas, cooked
2 cups chopped bell pepper (about 2 large)
1½ cups chopped onion (1 large)
1 (2 ounce) jar pimentos, drained
½ teaspoon minced garlic
1½ cups chopped jalapeno peppers (or one 16-ounce jar)
16 ounces zesty Italian dressing
Tortilla Chips

In a large bowl mix all ingredients. Refrigerate overnight. Serve at room temperature with chips. Makes approximately 7 cups or 50 1 tablespoon servings.

Nutty Cream Cheese Bars

PEGGY WILSON, HAWKINSVILLE, GA

1 (18 25-ounce) yellow or golden recipe cake mix
¾ cup melted butter
1½ cups chopped pecans, divided
1 cup packed light brown sugar
2 (8-ounce) packages cream cheese, softened
Vegetable Cooking Spray

Preheat oven to 350 degrees. Spray 9 x 13 baking pan with vegetable cooking spray. In medium bowl, combine the cake mix, melted butter and ¾ cup pecans over top. Bake for 25 to 30 minutes. Cool completely before slicing. Makes 36 bars.

Hamburger & Vegetable

MRS. BEATRICE SMITH, TENNILLE, GA

1 pint whole grain corn
1 pint butter beans
3 pints tomatoes, chopped or diced
1 pint chopped okra
1 pound ground beef
1 tablespoon finely chopped onions
1 tablespoon sugar
Salt and pepper to taste

Cook hamburger in pan with small amount of water, cook until brown and separated; then set aside.

Put vegetables and seasoning in pot. Cook for 45 minutes, to a low boil and stir often. Add hamburger to pot and cook for 15 minutes. Makes 4 to 6 servings.

Rose's Coconut Pie

ROSE HALL

4 eggs, well-beaten
½ cup self-rising flour
1¾ cups sugar
½ stick butter
1 teaspoon vanilla
2 cups buttermilk
1 can (or 16-ounce) bag of coconut

Preheat oven to 325 degrees. Mix all of the ingredients and pour into a two 9-inch glass pie plates. Bake for about 30 minutes. This pie will make it's own crust.

Pimento Cheese

WARREN BAPTIST CHURCH IN AUGUSTA

1 pound Kraft American Cheese (use this kind only)
⅓ cup milk
Combine the above and melt on low heat, stirring constantly. Remove from heat and cool.

Add:
3 tablespoons sugar
2 tablespoons vinegar
2 (4 ounce) cans or jars pimento, mashed
1 egg, beaten

Mix well, return to stove and cook on low for 6 or 7 minutes; stir; let cool. Add 1 pint Miracle Whip Salad Dressing (use this kind only).

Pear Relish

BEATRICE SMITH

1 peck pears (24 lbs. or 8 dry quarts)
3 cups sugar
6 large onions
1 tablespoon allspice
6 sweet green peppers
1 tablespoon salt
6 sweet red peppers
5 cups vinegar
1 bunch celery

Wash the pears, onions, peppers, and celery in cold water. Peel and core the pears, remove stems and seeds from the peppers. Clean the celery, peel the onions, and put them through a food chopper. Then add the sugar, allspice, salt and vinegar and let stand overnight. Heat to boiling.

Pack hot into jars, leaving ½ inch head space. Remove air bubbles. Wipe jar rims. Adjust lids. Process 20 minutes in a boiling water bath.

Or put all ingredients in large container when it comes to a boil — boil for 30 minutes. Put in sterilized jars and lids and seal. Makes 27 pints.

Pecans Dipped in Sunshine

1998 3RD PLACE 4-H JR. DIVISION
ASHLEY COVINGTON & APRIL BLACKSTOCK, FITZGERALD, GA

2 cups pecans, chopped
3 tablespoons butter, malted
3 (14-½ ounce) cans evaporated milk
2 (3-¾ ounce) packages instant vanilla pudding
2 ½ cups sugar
1 teaspoon vanilla flavoring
Approximately 2 quarts milk
Ice
Rock salt

Saute chopped pecans in melted butter, about 3 minutes, stirring constantly. Set aside to cool. Combine remaining ingredients in the ice cream churn and mix well. Add the sautéed nuts and stir thoroughly. Place the ice cream paddle (dasher) into the ice cream canister, cover with the lid and place in the bucket. Position the motor securely in place over the paddle and lock. Distribute crushed ice around the canister approximately ⅓ of the way up and pour ice creamsalt on top of the ice. Continue adding ice and ice cream salt until you reach the top of the canister. Plug in the motor and make sure the paddle is rotating in the canister. Add salt and ice as the ice in the bucket melts. Ice cream should freeze in approximately 20 minutes. When the motor quits running, the ice cream should be frozen. Remove the lid and serve.

Red Beans and Rice

1 pound red kidney beans, soaked
2 quarts water
2 tablespoons bacon drippings or corn oil
1 large onion, chopped
1 bunch green onions, chopped
1 bell pepper, seeded and chopped
4 cloves garlic, minced
1 pound smoked ham, cut into 1-inch cubes
3 bay leaves
1 teaspoon dried thyme leaves
2 tablespoons minced parsley
1 tablespoon dried thyme leaves
2 tablespoons minced parsley
1 tablespoon vinegar
2 teaspoons salt
1 teaspoon freshly ground black pepper
6 cups hot cooked white rice

Put the beans in a heavy soup pot with the water. Bring the water to a boil and turn down to a simmer. Simmer for 1 hour.

In a sauté pan, heat the bacon drippings and sauté the onion, green onions, bell pepper and garlic until they begin to color. Add to the bean pot.

In the same sauté pan, brown the smoked ham cubes. Add them and the bay leaves, thyme, parsley, vinegar, salt and pepper to the bean pot.

Simmer for another half hour, until the beans are tender and have made their own thick sauce of the liquid in the pot. Add water to the pot if the beans become too dry before they are completely cooked.

Stir occasionally while cooking to prevent the beans from sticking to the bottom of the pot. Do this carefully with a wooden spoon so you don't break the beans.

Adjust the seasonings, discard the bay leaves, and serve the beans spooned over the hot cooked rice.

Makes 6 servings as an entrée.

Swamp Gravy with hushpuppies & fish

Fry some fish golden brown. Pour off the grease, but leave some of the drippin's.

In the drippin's brown:
4 or 5 finely diced potatoes
2 or 3 finely diced onions
1 chopped bell pepper (optional)
When these are tender, add:
1 large can of tomatoes and 1 to 2 teaspoons of
    Louisiana Hot Sauce
Salt and pepper to taste

Pick some of the meat off 1 or 2 of the cooked fish and add to the mixture

Simmer for as long as you can stand the wonderful aroma. This is a basic recipe; anything can be added. Some people like corn or beans. If you really like it HOT, add 1 diced Jalapeño pepper.

Spaghetti Pie

1 pound ground beef
½ cup finely chopped onion
½ cup finely chopped green pepper
1 (14.5 oz) can diced tomatoes in their own juice
6-oz can tomato paste
¼ teaspoon sugar
¼ teaspoon Italian seasoning
4 ounces spaghetti, cooked according to
   package directions, drain well and set aside
2 tablespoons butter
2 eggs, slightly beaten
4 tablespoons butter
2 eggs, slightly beaten
4 tablespoons grated Parmesan cheese
Salt to taste

Preheat oven to 350 degrees. In a large skillet, combine ground beef, onion, and green pepper. Cook until ground beef is browned. Drain excess fat and add tomatoes, tomato paste, sugar and Italian seasoning. Simmer for 5 to 10 minutes (small amount of water may be added to keep mixture from sticking)

In a large bowl, combine butter, eggs. Parmesan and spaghetti, toss well. Place spaghetti mixture into a 10 to 10½-inch casserole dish and spread evenly; top with cottage cheese, spreading evenly. Add meat mixture, making sure to cover all of the spaghetti and cottage cheese. Bake for 20 to 25 minutes or until hot.* Top with mozzarella cheese and bake until cheese is melted.

*The spaghetti will form a crust. Do not allow pie to cook longer than 30 minutes or the eggs will begin to scorch. This recipe may be doubled. Makes 4 servings

The Absolute Best Vidalia Onion Rings

Several large sized Vidalia Onions
1 cup all purpose flour
1 teaspoon salt
1½ teaspoons baking powder
1 egg
¾ cup of milk
1 tablespoon salad oil

Slice large Vidalia Onions into rings. In one bowl, mix together flour, salt and baking powder. In another bowl, beat 1 egg yolk then stir in milk and salad oil. Add contents of bowl 2 to bowl 1, stirring until smooth. In third bowl, beat egg white until peaks form and fold into contents of bowl 1, stirring until smooth. Dip onion rings into batter and deep fry until golden brown.

You've no doubt seen in restaurants those beautiful onions that resemble tremendous chrysanthemums. The restaurants have a special tool that they use to make these appealing appetizers but here is a recipe that will help you make yours without the special tool. It is certainly a challenge and might be fun as a family project.

Squirrel Brunswick Stew
PROGRESSIVE FARMER/SEPTEMBER 1998

2 squirrels*, cut into serving pieces
2 quarts water
2 potatoes, diced
1 onion, chopped
1 cup corn
1 cup lima beans
1½ teaspoons salt
½ teaspoon black pepper
2 cups tomatoes
1½ teaspoons sugar
¼ cup butter or margarine

Place squirrel pieces in a large Dutch oven. Add water. Bring to a boil; reduce heat, and simmer 2 hours or until meat is tender, skimming surface occasionally. Remove meat from bones and return to liquid. Add all other ingredients except corn, and simmer 1 hour. Add corn and continue to simmer for 10 minutes. Serve 4 to 5.

*Chicken can be substituted for squirrel.

Vidalia Onion Casserole
WYNONA LEE STEPHENSON

2 tablespoons butter
2 tablespoons flour
1 cup chicken broth
1 can evaporated milk
3 cups wedged Vidalia onions
½ cup slivered almonds
½ teaspoons salt
½ teaspoons pepper
1 cup bread crumbs
½ cup grated cheese

Melt butter stir in flour, then add broth and canned milk. Cook stirring until it thickens and is smooth. Add drained onions, almonds, salt and pepper. Pour into buttered casserole dish (2 ½ quart size) cover with crumbs and cheese. Bake at 375 degrees for 30 to 40 minutes. Serves 6 to 8 people